Ab

Frontier Crusader for American Liberty

By Michael Crawley

Table of Contents

Introduction

The sixteenth president of the United States was a famous teller of stories. Throughout his boyhood, which he passed in poverty and isolation on the American frontier, Abraham Lincoln read as much of the written word as he could lay his hands on, borrowing newspapers, which were rare, and books, which were both rare and expensive, especially in his neck of the woods. Lincoln often made a point of memorizing the stories he read so that he could share them at social events with his neighbors, most of whom couldn't read for themselves. In this way, despite his virtually non-existent formal education, he began to develop the extraordinary reasoning and public speaking skills for which he became famous during his later political career.

One of Lincoln's favorite stories to tell was about a hero of the American Revolution, General

Ethan Allen, was won a famous victory at the Battle of Ticonderoga. Allen visited England in a diplomatic capacity after the war ended, and during his visit, he was invited to have dinner at the home of a wealthy and important Englishman. During the course of the meal, Allen excused himself to visit the privy. There, he discovered that his English host had hung a portrait of George Washington over the toilet. Allen returned to the dinner table and made no remark on his discovery of the portrait until his host asked him whether he had noticed it, and whether he thought it had been hung in a suitable location. Allen informed his host that he thought the location very suitable: "because nothing will make an Englishman sh-t quicker than the sight of General Washington."

Abraham Lincoln is generally remembered as a mournful individual, sagging somewhat under the weight of his office and the Civil War, which divided the country during his presidency. This is due in part to the famous photographs that were taken of Lincoln while he was president, revealing a gaunt face scored with deep worry lines, and eyes that are distant and distracted. It is probably also related to the fact that Lincoln suffered personal hardships during his time in the White House, including the death of his son Tad; his wife, Mary Todd Lincoln, suffered from serious mental illness and was nearly committed to a mental institution as a result of this loss.

Lincoln came from a very different background than most people who have been president of the United States. He did not come from privilege, or from a well connected family accustomed to wielding political power. The Lincoln family belonged to a new generation of Americans: frontiersmen and women who risked danger and suffered hardship to settle the sparsely inhabited lands on the western border of the rapidly expanding American nation. Lincoln's grandparents were of the Revolutionary generation, which founded the country, and lived in the eastern seaboard states. After the

Revolution, the country doubled its size, and settlers poured into the frontier country. Some of this land had been purchased from the Native American nations by treaty, but the majority was stolen from the Indians who lived there, resulting in terrible and bloody conflicts. The genocide of Native Americans was the ultimate result, and in the short term, isolated settler outposts faced attacks by angry tribes attempting to drive the white interlopers off their land. Lincoln's own family faced such an attack before Lincoln's birth, when his grandfather was murdered by a Native American wielding a tomahawk in front of his son, Lincoln's father.

The character of these nineteenth century Americans who settled the frontier was markedly different from those of their forbears who lived in the more cultivated towns and farmlands back east. Like Lincoln's family, they often lived in isolated log cabins and farmsteads, miles away from towns and settlements. They rarely had any kind of steady employment; they grew crops and kept livestock to supply their needs and sold the extra, if they had any. Schools were nearly nonexistent, and people had to travel miles to attend social gatherings, such as church meetings or political talks. Because of the isolation they faced, the constant grueling labor necessary to sustain their lives, lack of education, and constant danger, American frontiersmen were often harsh in their outlook, conservative in their views, and fatalistic in their acceptance of mortality and life's bleakness.

This general portrait of the character of frontier life is a fairly accurate depiction of Lincoln's own parents and relatives. Lincoln himself came to transcend his frontier upbringing in an extraordinary way, but the privations he faced in childhood marked him for the rest of his life. Lincoln was raised in terrible poverty, not just because he grew up in the backwoods of Kentucky and Illinois, but because his father was averse to exerting himself, and scarcely troubled to do more work than absolutely necessary to keep his family from starving. Thomas Lincoln actually sold Abraham into forced labor when Abraham was a teenager; common law in the early 19th century held that children were the property of their fathers until they were 21, and Thomas Lincoln took full advantage of his dominance over his son, sending Abraham to work as a field hand at neighboring farms and collecting all of his wages until Lincoln was legally an adult. Later in life, Lincoln would compare the years in which he was forced to work for his father's benefit to the plights of black slaves; his compassion for the plights of slaves, uncommon in the area of the country where he lived, was forged by his experience of this kind of powerlessness.

In addition to poverty and forced labor, Lincoln also knew the grief of watching his mother die of disease when he was a small boy; one of his earliest memories of childhood was of helping his father to carved pegs for his mother's coffin. When Lincoln was twenty, his sister, whom he loved dearly, died of complications in childbirth, which threw him into a depression that lasted nearly a year, resulting in strange changes in his behavior and even suicidal despondency. In speaking with a neighbor after her funeral, he asked, "What have I to live for?"—a question not easily answered, considering that no one could possibly have predicted the incredible heights he would rise to, once he had left the frontier life behind him.

Lincoln had an extremely keen mind, and from the time he was a small boy he had an avid desire to become educated. But on the Kentucky and Illinois frontier, schools were scarce, and the teachers not much better educated than their students. Teachers in frontier schools were not expected to know more than the basics of reading and writing, and rudimentary math— they were more likely to be hired for their ability to exert harsh discipline against their rowdy students. Lincoln attended two frontier schools for brief periods of time, but the vast majority of his education came from self directed study.

Lincoln's efforts to gain an education met with obstacles at every turn; not only were schools scarce and books difficult to obtain, but Lincoln's father actively opposed his reading habits. Thomas Lincoln considered Abraham "lazy" because he preferred reading to the endless grueling labor of subsistence farming. Lincoln had hopes even then of improving his lot in life by becoming a well educated man, but his father thought this a foolish dream. In Thomas Lincoln's opinion, education was a waste of time that could not possibly profit anyone. For a time, he even went so far as to beat Abraham if he caught him with a book, confiscating and destroying the books he had saved for so carefully or borrowed from neighbors. This, perhaps, has something to do with why, once Lincoln bade his family farewell to make his own way in the world at the age of twenty one, he never agreed to see his father again. He even refused to write him with news of his marriage and the births of his children. When Thomas Lincoln was on his deathbed, he sent word to his son through a relative, pleading for a visit; Lincoln coldly refused, telling the relative that he did not see how such a visit could be anything but distressing for either one of them. While this may seem harsh, it was probably an act of forbearance on Lincoln's part, permitting his father to pass away untroubled by the recriminations and accusations of cruelty and unfairness that Lincoln could justifiably have heaped on him.

In short, by the time Abraham Lincoln became president, he had faced trouble and adversity of a kind that his political colleagues—men who generally came from more privileged and sheltered backgrounds—could not possibly imagine. Because of his drive for self-improvement, his keen reasoning ability, his capacious and retentive memory, and his conviction that he could rely on no one but himself, he possessed far deeper learning than many men who went to the best schools and universities in America at the time. But he possessed a life long self consciousness of the differences between himself and his colleagues from more refined backgrounds, a self consciousness that translated to a deep humility, and a tendency, if not quite to underestimate himself, then certainly to make others underestimate him.

His rough upbringing revealed itself in small ways. Lincoln was not particularly appreciative of fine cuisine; he was said to eat his meals mechanically, and to take no more notice of bad food and bad cooking than of the best food prepared by the finest chefs. He was careless of how he dressed, which particularly irritated his wife, who came from a very wealthy family in the upper echelons of Lexington society; his cuffs tended to be frayed, his trousers too short for his famously long legs, and his necktie sloppily tied. Lincoln also had a fondness for bawdy stories and dirty jokes, as the story about General Allen perhaps demonstrates. Socially, he was ill at ease in the company of women, probably in part because the social graces he lacked put him at the greatest disadvantage there; in all male gatherings, he could tell his rude stories to general applause and laughter without fear of giving offense, but before ladies, he was fearful of making a gaffe that would offend their delicacy.

Abraham Lincoln was remembered by his friends and colleagues as a man of deep patience and infinite forbearance who dearly loved to laugh; this is a reflection on the maturity and generosity of his character, because he scarcely knew a period of unalloyed ease and happiness his whole life. The cruel hardships and parental abuse he endured until he was twenty one gave way to years of scrambling to make a living while keeping up his independent law studies. He faced disappointments in his early efforts to run for office. Lincoln lost his fiancé, Ann Rutledge, to illness when he was in his early twenties, and he was so despairing in the aftermath of this bereavement that his friends greatly feared he would take his own life, to the point that they compelled him to stay in their homes, and removed all sharp objects, such as razors and kitchen knives, from his reach.

Even after his political career began to prosper, he was to know little peace; his wife, whom he met and married in his late thirties, suffered from moderate to severe mood disorders and possibly other forms of mental illness, for which no diagnosis and no effective treatment existed in the nineteenth century. She had an unfortunate tendency to take out her sufferings, which were no doubt great, on her husband. Lincoln's friends declared that he did not have a single moment of peace or so much as an hour of domestic happiness in his marriage.

Compounding their unhappiness, the Lincolns lost three of their four sons. The death of their son Eddy, while the Lincolns were still living in Springfield, caused Lincoln extreme suffering;

their death of their son Tad, which occurred while Lincoln was president, grieved him even more deeply.

Despite the extraordinary difficulties in Lincoln's life, and despite the fact that he manifestly suffered from periods of intense mental affliction, to the point where he was susceptible to suicidal ideation, at least one eminent Lincoln scholar dissents from the sometimes simplistic characterization of Lincoln as a sufferer from clinical depression. Doris Kearns Goodwin, author of *Team of Rivals,* which studies the period of Lincoln's presidency in which he fought to get the Thirteenth Amendment passed, points to the remarkable activity that Lincoln was demonstrably capable of, even when the burdens he shouldered were at their heaviest. She also points to the fact that, far from having mood swings, he was noted for the constancy of his calm and resolute demeanor. Goodwin characterizes Lincoln's mental and emotional suffering as "melancholy", which, unlike clinical depression, is not a disease. People suffering from depression are generally paralyzed, unable to connect with their creativity or energy, unable to take action.

After a period of intense grieving over the death of Ann Rutledge, Lincoln took the advice of a friend who recommended that he throw himself entirely into his work, and thus managed to extricate himself from the temporary depression that made his friends fear he was suicidal. A person suffering from what we now understand to be clinical depression is rarely capable of this kind of self cure. If Lincoln's mind was affected by anything, it was probably the loss, neglect, and abuse he suffered as a child; the intense feelings of anxiety, despair, and sorrow created by hardships or mistreatment during a person's developing years can be triggered by events later in life, but are likely to be resolved when the trigger is removed and circumstances improve.

So what do we in the twenty first century think of, when we think of Lincoln? First comes the tall, gaunt, sad looking man in the dark suit and the stovepipe hat. Then, inevitably, comes slavery.

Slavery—the "peculiar institution", as it was known in the nineteenth century—dominated Lincoln's political career as a member of Congress, a founder of the Illinois Republican party, and as one half of the famed Lincoln vs Douglas debates, long before he became president. We associate Lincoln with the end of slavery in the same way we associate George Washington with winning the Revolutionary War. It is a legacy that in some way scarcely needs to be explained, but which, in other ways, and as tends to be the case with all of history's most popular figures, lives in our minds more as a mythology than as anything so mundane as historical biography. It is precisely because Lincoln's legacy as the liberator of the slaves is so storied that it needs to be examined carefully, and in context, by the discerning student of American history.

Apart from George Washington, Abraham Lincoln is probably America's most mythologized president. Take, for instance, the fulsome anecdotes and saccharine morality tales that have been spun out of his presidential origin story. For more than one hundred and fifty years, Lincoln's rise to the presidency has been touted as the epitome of the American dream. Anyone who knows anything about Lincoln knows that he overcame fantastic hardship as a young man; the fact that he later became president is therefore taken as proof that old fashioned hard work, determination, and ability can overcome literally any degree of difficulty or disadvantage.

The American frontier, the landscape which produced Lincoln, was legendarily the place where men who wished to become "self made" went to make something of themselves. From the earliest days of its founding, America has thought of itself as a meritocracy, a place where people of ability and ingenuity could accrue to themselves the honors that, in Europe, could only be inherited by the heirs of the aristocracy, even if they were entirely undeserving. Lincoln's biography fit this pattern perfectly—or at least, has been made to fit it. America is supposed to be the country where anyone can become president, and Abraham Lincoln, who, as legend has it, "was born in a log cabin that he built with his own hands", certainly seemed to qualify as "anyone".

Lincoln himself, however, is almost certainly the last person who would have approved of the American people mapping his life onto the dimensions of a ready made legend. While he was president, a man who wished to write a biography of Lincoln's life asked him to speak of his youth and childhood. Lincoln replied that there was simply nothing interesting to say about his early life. He had never liked discussing it, and apparently he had no very great desire for anything about it to be written down. When prompted for more detail, Lincoln quoted a line from the poem "Elegy Written in a Country Churchyard" by Thomas Gray, which he claimed summarized everything there was to know about the first 21 years of his life:

> Let not Ambition mock their useful toil,
>
> Their homely joys, and destiny obscure;
>
> Nor Grandeur hear with a disdainful smile,
>
> The short and simple annals of the poor.

The final line was the one which Lincoln quoted. Taken in context with the rest of the stanza, it would seem to imply that, while it would be unbecoming of the rich and powerful to condescend to the poor, the life of one poverty-stricken person is much like the life of another. He saw nothing particularly noble about his origins. On the contrary, he considered the poverty and backwoods isolation in which he had been raised to be peculiarly degrading, both intellectually and morally. In fact, Lincoln's early political career in the Illinois legislature focused particularly on public works projects such as railroads and canals, which linked the Great Lake to the Mississippi River. This was because he wanted to make it easier for Americans on the frontier to get from one place to another, for the extreme isolation of such backwoods settlements as the ones in which he grew up to come to an end. If Lincoln had felt that hardships of his upbringing had been worth the virtues of character they produced in him—which is the spin that is sometimes placed on his life story—it is doubtful that he would have devoted so much of his political life to lessening such hardships.

Lincoln's resentment of poverty was no doubt partly due to the fact that he got rather a late start in life, compared to most men in his line of work. At the age at which a young man in easier, softer circumstances would be finishing up his college education, or else starting out in a highly paid profession in which their way was eased by their family's social connections, Abraham Lincoln was "slaving" (as he put it) away for his father, and then working on a riverboat headed to New Orleans. While it is true that Lincoln's singular intelligence, his determination to better his condition, and his talents as a writer and public speaker enabled him to leave his father's hard-scrabble way of life behind forever, Lincoln would have been more than human if he had not wondered how much more he, with all his talents, might have accomplished, if he had not been held back from making his start for so many years, and if he had not had so much to make up for in terms of his education, breeding, and connections.

All of this is to say that the American public may have sentimentalized Abraham Lincoln's log cabin origins and rail-splitting youth, but Lincoln himself took no such rose-colored view of the life he had forsaken. He could not leave farming behind fast enough, and he always advised people over whom he had influence not to go into farming, unless they wanted to wreck their health and happiness. Still, he had been raised as a backwoods farmer, and he was far too humble to pretend to have come from more refined stock. As president, he frequently admitted to not knowing the correct spelling of words, and he always sought advice when he was unsure of his grammar. This shocked his secretaries, and sent a powerful message to his colleagues: if the President of the United States was not afraid to admit when he did not know something, neither should they be.

It is important to remember that Lincoln was the first Republican president. The Republican party had only been formed a decade or so before, with Lincoln amongst its first organizers in Illinois. In 1865, the Republican party was the party of strong central government, of support for a national bank, of federalist emphasis on the union over the sovereignty of states. Lincoln's governing political principle was that everyone deserved a fair shake—and his view of fairness involved using the power of the government to help people.

Lincoln knew better than most people how difficult it is to rise above poverty; and it is fair to wonder whether anyone less talented than Lincoln, who was in some ways a prodigy, could have made the leap in circumstances that he did. It is unlikely that he would have been impressed by modern politicians who cite him when arguing that there is no need for government programs to assist the poor, because the truly talented will always rise above their circumstances, as he did. The fact that he contemplated suicide on at least two occasions as a young man is proof that poverty exacts a devastating toll on a person's mental health; even with all his extraordinary talents, Lincoln stood in critical danger of failing to survive the suffering that such a life entailed.

Chapter One: Backwoodsman, Farmboy 1809-1831

The Lincoln Family

> If Nancy Hanks
> Came back as a ghost,
> Seeking news
> Of what she loved most,
> She'd ask first
> "Where's my son?
> What's happened to Abe?
> What's he done?"
>
> Rosemary Benet, 1933

Abraham Lincoln was named for his paternal grandfather, a captain in the Virginia militia during the Revolutionary War who moved his family from Virginia to Kentucky in 1782. This was an era during which Kentucky was still frontier territory, ruled by Indian tribes who had not given British colonists permission to settle there by treaty. Four years later, in 1786, the elder Abraham was shot and killed at his home by an unknown Indian, who was immediately killed in turn by the man's son, and the sixteenth president's uncle, Mordecai. Lincoln's father, Tom, a small child, witnessed the deaths. This bloody tale of his grandfather's ruthless execution was often repeated to Lincoln in his childhood, and seems to have made a distinct impression on him.

Lincoln's mother, Nancy Hanks, born in 1784, was the illegitimate child of a nameless but wealthy Virginia plantation owner, who, in Lincoln's own words, took "shameful" advantage of a poor teenage girl named Lucey Hanks, and refused to marry her afterwards. Little is known about Nancy's early life, save that she moved to Kentucky with her mother when she was a child, where she married Tom Lincoln in 1806. Nancy was known to be intelligent and hardworking, kind, and an excellent seamstress, able to earn money from her needlework. A portrait of her as a young woman reveals that Lincoln resembled his mother strongly. She gave birth to three children: Sarah, in 1807, Abraham, in 1809, and Tom, in 1811, who died in infancy. Nancy herself died of an illness contracted from drinking contaminated milk in 1818, at the age of 34, when Abraham was nine years old.

Tom Lincoln, born in 1778, was the fourth of five siblings. From the age of twelve, he had little adult support, being cut off by his brother Mordecai, who had inherited their father's property, and being hired out for work by his mother. Later in life, his trade was nominally carpentry, but he was rarely able to make much money from his work in a wild frontier country where people could scarcely afford to pay for skilled wood work. Tom Lincoln purchased a farm in 1803, but the soil was poor, and he did not live there with his new family after his marriage in 1806. Instead, Tom and Nancy Lincoln lived in Elizabethtown, Kentucky, for a short time before removing to a plot of land near Nolin Creek in 1807, where their son Abraham was born in a "miserable" log cabin two years later. When Abraham was two, the family moved to a farm on Knob Creek, and from there to Indiana, in 1816.

Tom Lincoln was considered by those who knew him to be a man of good morals and pleasant, even disposition, fond of story-telling, a trait he shared with his famous son. But Lincoln considered his father indolent, ignorant, and lacking industry. He perceived little resemblance between their characters; his own intelligence, drive, ambition, and ability to think in terms of far-reaching concepts and principles, he considered himself to have derived from his mother, whom he referred to as "a woman of genius".

Lincoln was never close to his father, who had little patience for his son's interest in reading and self-education. Rather inclined to take life as he found it, he too seemed to feel that he and Abraham did not have much in common; observers noted that he was inclined to treat his son harshly, beating him when he stepped out of line. As a bright child, Abraham had a tendency to correct his father in public, which Thomas couldn't abide. His treatment of Abraham was described as "inhuman" (the word meant something less severe than it does now in the nineteenth century). He considered Abraham's preoccupation with educating himself a waste of time, and sometimes threw away his son's books, which was particularly cruel, considering to what lengths Abraham had to go to obtain them.

Early Education

The poverty of Abraham Lincoln's childhood is legendary, and can scarcely be exaggerated; in the frontier country where he grew up, everyone was poor, and hard pressed to make ends meet. Lincoln's father in particular had an aversion to hard work that only compounded his impoverished condition. Frontier families put their children to work early; children of seven or eight had to help their parents with difficult chores around the home. Boys were expected to plow and hunt, at the very least. For this reason, possibly, Lincoln did not especially enjoy talking about his early years, feeling that there was not much to say about them that could not be summed up by declaring that his family had been "the very poorest of people." He remembered having shoes that bared his toes to the winter chill, and coats that were "out at the elbows". His extended family remained poor throughout his life, and frequently applied to him for money after he moved to the city of Springfield and began to earn a reputation as a successful lawyer.

Because of his father's poverty and disdain for learning, as well as the remoteness of the country where he lived, Lincoln had very little in the way of any formal education. He was known to remark later in life that the number of days he spent in a school room added up to less than a year. Even if his father had been more amenable to his scholarly pursuits, it is doubtful whether his formal education would have been much better. Schools on the frontier were few and far between, and attendance was not free. Furthermore, the teachers who ran them were only slightly more educated than their pupils. Frontier school teachers were not expected to know more than the barest rudiments of reading, writing, and "ciphering to the rule of three"—a method of mathematical calculation in which three numbers are set in a row, and the student has to figure out the fourth in the sequence. The one-room log cabins that functioned as the schoolhouses had neither floors nor windows. The students were frequently beaten with sticks and bundles of twigs at the teacher's whim.

Lincoln is famous for commenting that as a young man he had made an effort to borrow and read every book he could find within fifty miles of his home, a claim which might be exaggerated, but which certainly represents the essential truth of his education, which was that he had to make a special effort to expand his knowledge beyond the rudiments of reading and writing. He declared that by the age of twenty one he had only mastered basic reading and arithmetic, though he took a life long interest in correcting his irregular spelling. Lincoln was particularly fond of mathematics, and while he was president he learned by heart the first six volumes of Euclid (the ancient Greek philosopher who set down the principles of geometry). As a boy, he was known to be fond of the famous (and somewhat fabricated) biography of George Washington written by Parson Weems; it may have been Weems' idealized accounts of Washington's youthful efforts to educate himself that inspired Lincoln to copy out sections from books that interested him. The Bible, *Robinson Crusoe*, *Aesop's Fables*, and *Pilgrim's Progress* are among the books that Lincoln would have had access to as a child.

By dint of constant practice, Lincoln developed good handwriting, an extremely rare skill in the frontier country. This led directly to his developing a facility for composition: when his neighbors learned that he had the skill of writing formal letters and drafting legal documents, they applied to Lincoln to write letters on their behalf. From this practice, he learned to listen to people's stories and troubles and translate them into moving appeals to lawyers and tradesmen and government officials. He was also called upon to read letters, books, and newspapers to his illiterate neighbors. Lincoln was described by one of these neighbors as having a fiercely retentive memory, often memorizing what he read.

Sarah Bush Johnston Lincoln

Lincoln may have had the misfortune to lose his mother at a young age, and his father may have spurned his company, but he was lucky in his step-mother, who came to live with the Lincoln family in December of 1819, more than a year after Nancy Hanks' death. Ten years younger than Tom Lincoln, Sarah Bush Johnston had been married once before and had given birth to three children in her first marriage. When Sarah Lincoln met her new step-children for the first time, she was shocked by how ragged and wild they looked. Young Sarah and Abraham had been without a mother for fifteen months, and during that time their father had frequently abandoned them to fend for themselves while he went away from home on business. Sarah Lincoln—described as "a poor woman, but of spotless character"—quickly took the children in hand and effected marvelous changes in the Lincoln household, converting what had been little more than a shack made of logs into a house with decent furniture and kitchen utensils.

Sarah Lincoln was the first person to pay real attention, not only to young Abraham's emotional needs, but to his intellectual ambitions. She spotted right away that he was a boy of uncommon intelligence and talents. And unlike Abraham's father, who perceived these attributes as failings to be beaten out of him, she encouraged Abraham's reading and his efforts at self-improvement. Later in her life, she said of her step-son that he "never gave me a cross word or look, and never refused in fact, or even in appearance, to do anything I requested him." Lincoln reciprocated her high opinion, and declared her the best friend he had ever had. Abraham and his sister Sarah also became close to their step-mother's son and two daughters from her first marriage, and it was often remarked that the whole family were as affectionate toward one another as if they had all been the children of the same parents.

Adolescence and Young Adulthood

By the time he was a teenager, Lincoln had grown enormously tall, and was commonly described as awkward, gangly, and even ugly. Nonetheless, he was good-natured, and whenever he was teased about his looks, he would laugh along with the joke. He seemed to have little interest in the opposite sex; it was thought that he considered the girls in his neighborhood too frivolous to have a conversation with, though he might also have been considering the future of his career. If he had married early, it would have been difficult to pursue the further education he desired. At county balls, Lincoln often held court with the other men, exchanging news and telling stories, which irritated the young women because there was no one left to dance with them.

When Lincoln was sixteen, his father Thomas ran into significant financial trouble, when a friend whose loan he had insured defaulted on payment. Thomas Lincoln's solution was to hire Abraham out to his neighbors as a kind of field hand, for about ten cents a day. All of Abraham's wages which went directly to Thomas. Children were considered the property of their fathers under the laws of the time, and while renting

them out for work as Thomas did was considered harsh treatment, it was not at all unheard of. (Lincoln's grandmother, in fact, had done the same to Thomas Lincoln when he was as young as twelve.) Referring to this period of his life, Lincoln later remarked that he had once "been a slave" himself. He was put to work doing a number of taxing jobs: clearing fields, operating a ferry, and butchering hogs, among other things. When his day's work was over, Lincoln lay awake in bed until midnight, reading whichever book he had recently managed to get hold of.

During this period of his life, Lincoln took a job working on a cargo boat trip to Louisiana. This involved a dangerous but eventful trip down the Mississippi river to areas of the country Lincoln had never visited before, trading cotton, tobacco, and sugar. (It was during this trip that Lincoln was exposed to slavery and the slave trade, possibly for the first time in his life: he happened to pass by an auction block where black women were stripped of clothing and inspected by buyers, a sight that Lincoln called "a disgrace".) Lincoln took to the water to such an extent that he considered joining the crew of some ship and running away from the virtual indentured servitude in which he was laboring for his father's gain. He was legally bound to his father until the age of twenty-one, however, and his relatives advised him against bringing legal trouble on himself by attempting escape.

In 1829, Lincoln's twentieth year, he seemed to grow especially sensitive to the injustice of his situation, resulting in a period of uncharacteristic black moods and malicious feelings towards some of his neighbors. His anxiety and strange behavior was exacerbated when his beloved sister Sarah, who had married some eighteen months before, died in childbirth. Lincoln had already been at odds with her husband's family, accusing them of abusing her, and when she died he blamed them for not seeking a doctor to attend her during the birth.

His grief at his sister's passing was intense. Lincoln, characteristically, did not provoke a physical fight with the family, but instead turned to his pen, writing a "sharp" and "cutting" satire on the marriage of his former brothers in law, which became a popular piece of entertainment in the neighborhood. While it drew attention to Lincoln's intellectual attainments, it was considered out of character for the young Abraham to write something so harsh about a neighbor, and was considered evidence that he was in a dark frame of mind after his sister's passing.

Illinois

In 1830, Thomas Lincoln moved with some thirteen members of his immediate and extended family from Indiana to Illinois, near Decatur. Lincoln turned twenty-one on February 12, 1830, making him a legal adult and no longer bound to work for his father. But despite his fervent wish to get away from his father's control, he elected to continue working on his family's behalf for awhile, until he was sure they were comfortably settled in their new home. He worked for neighbors, doing the same jobs he had performed for families in Indiana, and acquired a reputation as a famous "rail splitter", someone who could chop wood for a fence fast and well.

Back in Indiana, Lincoln had taken a strong interest in local politics—reading newspapers, attending campaign speeches, and acquiring perspectives on the issues of the day. Lincoln himself had begun to develop a taste for public speaking, which he practiced at small social gatherings; he had a reputation as a storyteller that would follow him throughout his political career. In Illinois, he made a name for himself early by attending a political debate and standing up after the candidates had given their speeches and making a speech himself which was deemed better than either of those given by the men running for office. Afterwards, one of the candidates asked Lincoln how he had learned so much. Lincoln was still a very poor, very young man, shabbily dressed in buckskin, and the appearance of education and understanding in such a person was remarkable. The politician encouraged Lincoln to continue his studies and try to make something of himself.

Lincoln appears to have taken this advice seriously. His family, after a hard year involving outbreaks of malaria, followed by blizzards and deep snow, moved back to Indiana in 1831, but Lincoln did not go with them. He had had enough of farming for a lifetime, and was determined to find a way of making his living that did not involve tedious, endless labor for little profit.

Lincoln's feelings on parting with some members of his family might have given him pain, but he seems to have felt little besides relief at escaping what he called the "parental tyranny" of his father. After they parted ways in 1831, there was little further contact between them. Lincoln never visited his father or allowed him to meet his grandchildren, although he supported his step-mother Sarah from his father's death to the end of his life.

Chapter Two: Postmaster, Legislator, Lawyer 1831-1837

Boatman and Shop Clerk

After setting out from his father's home with all his possessions tied up in a bundle which he carried at the end of a stick, Lincoln returned to his earlier plan of earning a living by his skills as a waterman, signing up for a second trip down the Mississippi to Louisiana. Afterwards, he was offered a job as the clerk of a small shop and mill in New Salem, Illinois, by the owner of the boat, who was greatly impressed with Lincoln's capabilities. Lincoln embarked on this new career in the autumn of 1831; he was delighted to have a job that paid well but did not require hard physical labor. It was during his tenure as a shopkeeper that Lincoln first earned the nickname "Honest Abe", due to his reputation for scrupulous integrity in business dealings.

Lincoln desired a relatively short working day that did not tire him too much physically because he had, by this time, set his sights on a career in law. Most young men who studied for the law had college educations and social connections in high society, but Lincoln, whose education was extremely limited, recognized that he would have to work very hard on his own in order to meet the required standard. He spent the next five years reading and studying during his leisure time in order to make up the deficiencies in his learning. He began his studies with a focus on English grammar, a necessary measure for a man with a thick Kentucky accent and a backwoods dialect. He also read histories, biographies, and literature, including the plays of Shakespeare and the poetry of Alexander Pope, though he did not care for novels.

In 1832, Lincoln joined the Literary and Debating Society of New Salem. Lincoln had a reputation as a famous teller of humorous stories, but at these informal debates, he displayed equal skill in making serious speeches and engaging in political debates. In a short time, he became known as the best debater in the county, holding forth on such topics as slavery, temperance, votes for women, and other local political issues important to the inhabitants of Illinois.

Lincoln's First Bid for Public Office

From April to July of 1832, Lincoln was a volunteer during what is known as the Black Hawk War, in which a band of some eight hundred Native Americans from different nations banded together in an attempt to drive white settlers off tribal lands in northern Illinois. His regiment did not see battle, but he gained valuable military experience as the captain of his regiment. After mustering out, Lincoln returned to New Salem, where some of his friends from the Debating Society urged him to run for the Illinois State Legislature.

Lincoln wrote a lengthy essay announcing his candidacy—the first of many political papers he would author in his career—in which he outlined his views on the necessity of a strong central government. This position placed him in opposition to Democrat president Andrew Jackson, who favored minimal government. The following is an excerpt from the conclusion of the essay:

"Considering the great degree of modesty which should always attend youth, it is probable I have already been more presuming than becomes me. However, upon the subjects of which I have treated, I have spoken as I thought. I may be wrong in regard to any or all of them; but holding it a sound maxim, that it is better to be only sometimes right, than at all times wrong, so soon as I discover my opinions to be erroneous, I shall be ready to renounce them.

"Every man is said to have his peculiar ambition. Whether it be true or not, I can say for one that I have no other so great as that of being truly esteemed of my fellow men, by rendering myself worthy of their esteem. How far I shall succeed in gratifying this ambition, is yet to be developed. I am young and unknown to many of you. I was born and have ever remained in the most humble walks of life. I have no wealthy or popular relations to recommend me. My case is thrown exclusively upon the independent voters of this county, and if elected they will have conferred a favor upon me, for which I shall be unremitting in my labors to compensate. But if the good people in their wisdom shall see fit to keep me in the back ground, I have been too familiar with disappointments to be very much chagrined."

Lincoln would one day be famous for the profundity and wisdom of speeches, and while this early effort might be somewhat lacking in comparison to them, it is nonetheless a remarkable piece of writing considering that at this point in Lincoln's life he had scarcely had a conversation with a literate person, and had learned everything he knew about writing and rhetoric from the comparatively small number of books he had been able to read while working on his father's behalf.

The speech seems to have made an excellent impression on the residents of New Salem. All that summer, Lincoln campaigned throughout Sangamon County, giving speeches at public gatherings. While he lost this election, owing largely to the fact that he was little known in other parts of the state, he won 277 of the 300 votes cast in New Salem itself. Lincoln was encouraged by the results, and determined to run again in two years' time.

In May of 1833, Lincoln was appointed the official United States postmaster of New Salem, Illinois, owing largely to the fact that he was one of very few people in the town who could read and write well enough to qualify for the position. He kept the position until he moved to the city of Springfield in 1836, but as the work was only part time and the pay poor, he was obliged to do other work as well, including surveying. As a surveyor, he marked out plots of land for homes, schools, and businesses, as well as entire new towns.

Early Career in Politics and Law

In 1834, Lincoln once again ran for a seat in the Illinois legislature; this time, he won. His success in this election was due to several factors. For one thing, despite the fact that he opposed the politics of the dominant Democratic party, the local Democrats supported his candidacy, because they preferred him to his friend and rival, John Todd Stuart, who was also running. (The woman Lincoln would go on to marry, Mary Todd, was Stuart's cousin.)

Lincoln also had the good fortune of forming a close, supportive friendship with an educated and influential North Carolina transplant by the name of Bowling Green, who took it upon himself to foster Lincoln's efforts at self-education. It is perhaps a sign of how highly Green esteemed Lincoln that he encouraged the younger man to seek public office, despite the fact that Lincoln was a Whig and Green was a Democrat. Knowing that Lincoln was interested in studying law, Green invited Lincoln to attend legal proceedings and court cases which he presided over as a justice of the peace. Green allowed Lincoln to study from his law books, and Lincoln even gained preliminary experience in presenting cases to the court under Green's presiding—lawyers were scarce in the area, and the skills even of a man of Lincoln's limited knowledge of the law were in demand.

Initially intimidated by the fact that preliminary learning in subjects such as Latin, Greek, French, rhetoric, and logic were considered essential to the study of law, Lincoln eventually came to understand that many lawyers and judges in Illinois had attended neither law school nor college. According to Allen Clough, a resident of Illinois and contemporary of Lincoln's, becoming a lawyer in the American west was not very difficult: "an ordinary intelligent man with a moderate education can be admitted [to the bar] in about one year." Lincoln, of course, did not have even a moderate education, but by borrowing law books from Stuart and Green, and purchasing others cheaply at auctions and estate sales, he learned all that was required by studying on his own. In 1836, Lincoln became a lawyer by obtaining a "certificate of good moral character" and a license, and by taking an oral examination administered by a Justice Lockwood of the Illinois Supreme Court.

Later in life, when other young men interested in taking up the law asked him how best to go about studying it, Lincoln replied with a list of titles of law books and recommended that they forego formal instruction at a law school or another attorney's office, and simply read until they had mastered all the necessary principles. Lincoln, of course, was extraordinarily self-motivated and had more than enough ambition to fuel his independent studies; he was sometimes less than sympathetic towards young people who were not equally ambitious.

When Lincoln took up his seat in the Illinois General Assembly in 1834, he was still so poor that he couldn't even afford a decent suit of clothes, and had to borrow the money for a new outfit from one of his wealthy constituents. At this time, the capital of Illinois, and therefore the seat of the Assembly, was the town of Vandalia, a relatively unpopulated establishment that was nonetheless full of bustling social life compared to Lincoln's home of New Salem. Lincoln's first year in the Assembly was relatively quiet. He sponsored an unsuccessful bill that proposed to limit the jurisdiction of justices of the peace, and later, a successful bill to construct a toll bridge over a body of water known as Salt Creek. His chief interest during the 1834-1835 session was to watch and learn how the business of politics was conducted, but he became known to other members for his literary prowess, and was often asked to help draft other people's bills.

First Romance

Lincoln became briefly engaged in 1835 to a young woman by the name of Ann Rutledge. Lincoln had briefly been a lodger at her father's tavern in 1831, though he was living elsewhere by the time they began courting. Rutledge was described by those who knew her as small, neat, pretty, and clever, exceptionally skilled at spinning and needlework, and possessing an appetite for education and improving her mind. She had become engaged to a wealthy local merchant around the time that she and Lincoln first met, but in 1834 he went on a long trip to New York, and his letters to Rutledge were so infrequent that she believed he had forgotten her. The other young women of New Salem regarded her as having been deserted by her fiancé, which made her the subject of pity and gossip, and it is believed that Lincoln began escorting her to social events because he felt sorry for her. Their mutual seriousness of mind, regard for education, and desire to improve their social stations made them an eminently compatible couple, and Lincoln eventually proposed to her.

A tentative wedding date was set for a year later; Rutledge wanted to complete another year of school before she married, and Lincoln, who was still very poor, wished to complete his law studies and be admitted to the bar. Rutledge also wanted to wait until her former fiancé returned home from his trip, so that she could speak to him in person about the fact that she considered their engagement ended by his behavior. However, in the summer of 1835, Rutledge became ill with typhus; she died after a few weeks, on August 25.

Lincoln was reportedly much affected and depressed by Ann Rutledge's death. Some of his friends believed that he felt such deep grief upon losing her that he was in danger of losing his sanity. He was known to take long walks in the woods alone with his gun, supposedly to hunt. He evidently admitted that he had considered committing suicide, and as a result his friends took turns making Lincoln stay at their homes, where they could keep an eye on him. Eventually, Lincoln took the advice of a friend who declared that work was the best cure and distraction for deep grief; he began throwing himself into his study of the law with a renewed energy, and by December of that year he was well enough to attend the General Assembly.

Illinois and Michigan Canal Act

The special session of the Illinois General Assembly met in the winter of 1836-1836 to discuss a plan known as the Illinois and Michigan Canal Act, a public works program that was intended to boost commerce and trade in Illinois by linking Lake Michigan to the Mississippi River, thus making it easier for merchants to transport their goods south and east. Lincoln, whose Whig politics were Federalist in their sympathies, was strongly in favor of such government funded programs, and the measure passed by a slim margin. This was the first political battle between north and south that Lincoln would be involved in: northern Illinois versus southern Illinois, that is, with the wealthier merchant class settlers of the north favoring the canals program, while the poorer subsistence farmers of the south opposing the program on the grounds that it would open Illinois to interference from "Yankees" (the word referred to Americans from the north-east.) The canal program was not completed until about 1847.

Re-election

In 1836, Lincoln ran for another term in the General Assembly and was elected first out of the seventeen candidates on the ticket. By this time, his political identity was more fully formed, and he was considered a leader amongst the Whigs. (The conservative, small-government party in the early 1800's was the Democratic party, while the party favoring progressive reform and Federalist principles of strong central government took the name "Whig" from the British political system. In later decades, by the time Lincoln was president, this party would re-organize under the name of the "Republican" party. This distinction is important for the modern reader to note, as the two parties effectively swapped names by the mid twentieth century.)

Lincoln was beginning to earn a name for himself with his pen—not just for the literary skill that made his colleagues turn to him to compose bills, but for his sharp sense of humor and his penchant for political satire. Lincoln published a number of humorous articles in local newspapers such as the Sangamon *Journal,* belittling Democratic politicians and making them look ridiculous. He was likewise known as the most effective public speaker on the Whig side, the best able to rein in his temper and devastate his opponents with sarcasm. This was a considerable change from Lincoln's first term, during which he had been fairly reserved, listening more often than speaking.

One of the projects supported by the Democratic party which Lincoln particularly opposed (and satirized in print) was the system of a nominating convention for presidential candidates. Prior to this point, any man over the legal age required by the Constitution could simply announce his candidacy and his name would appear on the ballot. The convention, in which party leaders choose the candidate that the entire party is expected to support, was the invention of Democrat politicians Ebenezer Peck and Stephen A. Douglas, the latter of whom Lincoln would famously oppose in a series of debates later in his career. Writing satirically under a pseudonym, Lincoln questioned whether "six men can regulate the affairs of Fulton County better than six hundred".

The Illinois State Bank

One of the most hotly contested subjects between pro government Federalists and their small government opponents since the founding of the United States had been the existence of the national bank. Established by Alexander Hamilton during George Washington's first term as president, it was immediately opposed by Thomas Jefferson, who believed that if the federal government assumed the debts of individual states (thereby assuming the power to collect taxes from the states to pay the debt down), it would pave the way for monarchist factions to undermine the democratic government in the nation's future. The debate was still ongoing in the 1830's, and by 1835 the anti Federalist president Andrew Jackson had effectively dismantled the Bank of the United States. A new central bank for the state of Illinois, which had been chartered in 1835, was a subject of continuous debate during the 1836-1837 legislative session.

One of the most famous speeches of Lincoln's early legislative career was delivered in defense of the state bank. He supported the bank on the grounds that it strengthened currency, and also because he had found that the ordinary people of Illinois had seen only good things come out of the bank's founding. Lincoln held the traditional and well supported view that central banks strengthened the credit of, and fostered economic growth in, the state that supported them. Lincoln was also a passionate proponent of public works projects, such as the one that funded the Illinois and Michigan Canal Act, and others that promoted the building of railroads. He saw these building projects as a way of linking the scattered frontier settlements together. Having grown up in an extremely isolated backwoods area himself, Lincoln felt that such isolation was harmful to the people who lived in those areas. A well designed infrastructure would decrease the isolation of these settlements; and a central bank was crucial to funding such an infrastructure. It also made it easier for the poor to get credit, another cause dear to Lincoln's political heart. Despite Lincoln's efforts, however, the Democrats in the assembly succeeded in closing the bank for a year to undergo an examination of its lending policies.

A New State Capital

In 1836, the capital city of Illinois was Vandalia, which, as we discussed earlier, was not much of a city. Its population was small, and while it was a thriving center for commerce in comparison to such rural hamlets as New Salem, where Lincoln was from, it was rapidly being dwarfed by newer and more populous cities in the north of Illinois. Vandalia had been chosen as the state capital at a time when the southern part of Illinois was much more densely populated by settlers, but in more recent decades, the building of canals (such as the famous Eerie canal) had attracted larger numbers to northern cities such as Springfield and Chicago. By law, Vandalia had to remain the capital of Illinois until 1839, but after that the field was clear for another city to be chosen. In addition to Vandalia's remote location, which made it difficult for legislators to travel over muddy roads from other parts of the state, it was considered an unhealthy place to live for any length of time, close to swamps, and therefore mosquitoes, which spread diseases such as malaria, or the "ague", an illness which wreaked havoc on settler populations during this era.

Advocating for the city of Springfield as the new capital of Illinois would become Lincoln's chief legislative agenda during the 1836-1837 session of the Assembly. He was, in fact, the head of the pro Springfield legislative delegation, despite the fact that he was a relative newcomer to the assembly. Springfield was located in Sangamon County, where Lincoln and the other delegates were from, and theirs was the largest county delegation in the legislature; this meant that they had considerable power to make deals and trade favors, since, all together, they commanded a large number of votes. (The Sangamon County delegates, all of whom were over six feet tall, were nicknamed by their Democrat opponents as "the Long Nine.") This was one of Lincoln's first major opportunities to demonstrate his talent for playing the game of politics—promising support for other politicians' pet projects in exchange for their support for naming Springfield the new capital. As it happened, most of the projects that other members of the assembly wanted support for were just the kind of internal improvement projects, building railroads, canals, and better roads, that Lincoln was highly in favor of in the first place, which gave him an advantage in the bargaining process.

In the end, after an unsuccessful attempt by anti Springfield delegates to redraw county lines so that Sangamon County (and thus its delegates) was split in half, Lincoln made a successful proposal to the legislature that ensured Springfield would be chosen as the new capital. He, or rather, his committee, suggested that whichever city was chosen as the new capital should be responsible for donating two acres of land, as well as the funds for constructing the capital building. Springfield, as it happened, was the only one of the cities vying for the capital that was wealthy enough to support the construction project. Lincoln came close to defeat at several points in the negotiation process, at one point confessing to a friend that he had made every bargain it was in his power to make and still had not got the support he needed. But by making some last minute amendments to the bill that quieted the concerns of some of those who had been opposed to it, Lincoln managed a victory of 46 votes for to 37 against in February of 1837.

Lincoln's political finesse throughout the Springfield-Vandalia debate impressed his colleagues in the legislature to such a degree that they began to consider him one of the foremost political talents of their acquaintance; his name began to be mentioned as a possible future candidate for governor.

Lincoln's First Stand Against Slavery

In 1837, Lincoln, for the first time in his political career, came to grapple with slavery, the issue which would define his legacy. Unlike his efforts to secure Springfield as the new capital of Illinois, his stance on slavery would make him anything but universally popular.

In March, the Illinois legislature had passed resolutions stating that they were opposed to the formation of abolitionist, or anti-slavery societies. The resolutions were prompted by a pamphlet which had been published the previous year by a major abolitionist society back east, describing atrocities perpetrated by southern slave owners, and calling for slavery to be abolished in Washington, D.C. The legislatures of the southern states had reacted with outrage, and the Illinois legislature has passed its resolutions to express solidarity with them. Although slavery was not legal in Illinois, many of its settlers were transplants from the south, and anti-black prejudice was rampant.

Lincoln's response to the resolution was simple, but profound: he wrote a protest, which he showed to a number of other delegates, and asked if anyone would sign it with him. Only one person, a fellow Sangamon County delegate and native of Vermont named Dan Stone, agreed to do so. In the protest, Lincoln declared that "slavery is founded on both injustice and bad policy". In the 1830's, voicing any degree of anti slavery sentiment was a deeply unpopular and risky move—not just in the south or on the frontier, but anywhere in the nation. The southern states maintained that abolitionists agitated slaves and provoked them to violent rebellions in which they massacred their white owners. Even in states where slavery was not legal, such as Illinois, white citizens tended to believe that slaves were naturally violent and immoral, and that if they were free they would wreak destruction on the country.

Lincoln's stance was therefore a bold one, and since it can have gained him nothing politically, it must be attributed wholly to his moral feeling that slavery was wrong. This was not enough to make him an abolitionist, or put him beyond the pale of what his colleagues in the assembly would be willing to tolerate, but it gives us an idea of his character, and the ideals he would carry into his later political career. Not long after Lincoln penned this protest, Springfield only narrowly averted a mob uprising when word got around that a Presbyterian church intended to host a sermon preaching against slavery. Afterwards, the town of Springfield adopted a set of resolutions declaring that abolitionists were fanatics, that to espouse anti slavery doctrines was tantamount to wishing whites in the south dead at the hands of murderous slaves, and that abolitionism was inconsistent with the tenets of Christianity. All of this goes to show how entrenched slavery was in the minds of the American people in the decades prior to the Civil War, and how deeply unpopular were Lincoln's modest feelings that slavery was unjust.

Yet even as Lincoln protested the Illinois assembly's pro-slavery stance, he distanced himself from the name of "abolitionist". In the minds of most people, "abolitionist" was synonymous with "troublemaker", and Lincoln, a shrewd politician first and foremost, avoided such loaded labels. In the protest document he presented to the Illinois legislature, he expressed the opinion that abolitionism compounded the evils of slavery, declaring that he could not "conceive how any true friend of the black man can hope to benefit him through the instrumentality of abolition societies." In other words, Lincoln felt that abolitionist societies, by stirring up heated feelings and frightening slave owners, actually made it more difficult to advance the cause of ending slavery by legal means. This was a popular view even amongst fairly progressive thinkers at the time. While hard line abolitionists believed that every person who was not a slave owner had a duty to rebuke the practice of slavery wherever they encountered it, moderate anti slavery thinkers held the view that if not for abolitionists stirring up trouble, slavery would eventually come to a natural end in many of the southern states that were not as economically dependent on slavery as those in the deep south. In later decades, there was even a strong feeling that abolitionists were responsible for provoking the Civil War, because they had forced the south to defend its interests rather than trying to work with them.

Lincoln's political stance on slavery, both during the 1830's and later on, was more conciliatory than any true abolitionist would have stood for;

he believed, as he remarked in a speech on temperance in 1842, that "a drop of honey catches more flies than a gallon of gall." In order to win people to his way of thinking, he believed it necessary to convince them that he would look after their interests, which was more difficult to do with a self-righteous attitude. Only by tact and compromise could contentious and controversial political reforms be carried out. With regards to ending slavery in the District of Columbia, the issue which had sparked the Illinois legislature's resolution and Lincoln's protest, Lincoln believed it should be done, but only with the consent of the voters.

Chapter Three: A Lawyer in Springfield 1837-1843

The Law Firm of Lincoln and Todd

In March of 1837, Abraham Lincoln officially registered as a lawyer with the Illinois Supreme Court. About this time, Lincoln moved from New Salem to Springfield, which, despite the qualities which had made it a suitable candidate to replace Vandalia as the state capital, was nonetheless a remarkably gloomy and unprepossessing village, notorious for its inconveniently muddy roads. Lincoln had some minor debts at the time, which he paid by selling his horse, and he was invited to live with a friend by the name of William Butler until he found a way to make his living. The meager pay he drew from serving in the legislature had been spent already, and he had no immediate way of earning any more now that the legislature was no longer in session. Lincoln would take his meals at the Butler home for the next five years, while boarding with another friend by the name of Joshua Speed.

Around this same time, Lincoln established a law firm in partnership with the man who had helped him get elected to the legislature a few years before, John Stuart Todd. Most of the business the small firm dealt with in its early years had to do with petty squabbles between poor farmers who were fighting over the ownership of livestock. The average fee charged was about five dollars. Lincoln and Todd did business, not merely in Springfield, which would not have supplied them with enough business to make ends meet, but in an area comprising ten counties. Lincoln dealt with the majority of the firm's clients; both he and Todd saw their law practice merely as a way to earn a living while their political careers became established, and Todd, as the senior partner, was away most of the time pursuing election to Congress.

In Lincoln's first major case, he defended a man named Truett against a murder charge. Truett had shot and killed a political opponent by the name of Early. Despite Truett's obvious guilt, the jury acquitted him, owing largely to the strong closing argument delivered by Lincoln. The law firm of Lincoln and Todd earned five hundred dollars from the case, the most money they ever made from a client while they were in practice.

The Election of 1838

Lincoln's seat in the Illinois legislature was up for re-election in 1838, and the same election saw John Stuart Todd running for Congress. The financial Panic of 1837, which had endangered the Illinois State Bank, had turned the tide of public feeling against the Democratic party, and Lincoln and Todd both stood to benefit, as they were Whigs. Todd's opponent in this election was Stephen A. Douglas, and Lincoln did battle on his friend's behalf using the weapon which had made his reputation in New Salem: satirical essays full of political invective, published anonymously in the newspapers.

In response to certain articles which had been published in favor of Douglas, Lincoln gave the most famous speech of his early career, entitled "The Perpetuation of Our Political Institutions", an address delivered to the Young Men's Lyceum of Springfield. Lincoln addressed a number of issues in this address, including the fact that in recent years there had been a growing tendency towards mob violence all over the United States, concluding in lynching (the kidnapping and hanging of a person in retribution for some perceived wrongdoing.) The main thrust of his argument was a sly allusion to Douglas, which, without naming him, characterized him as a tyrant in the making, comparing him to politicians from history who, in pursuit of recognition for their talents and abilities, had not been content to gain power by democratic means.

The following excerpt from the Lyceum address provides an excellent example of Lincoln's extraordinary ability, even in the early years of his career, to compose elegant phrases and deliver stirring rhetoric that could sway audiences to support the cause he was championing:

"Many great and good men, sufficiently qualified for any task they should undertake, may ever be found whose ambition would aspire to nothing beyond a seat in Congress, a gubernatorial, or a presidential chair; but such belong not to the family of the lion or the tribe of the eagle. What! think you these places would satisfy an Alexander, a Caesar, or a Napoleon? Never! Towering genius disdains a beaten path. It seeks regions hitherto unexplored. It sees no distinction in adding story to story upon the monuments of fame erected to the memory of others. It denies that it is glory enough to serve under any chief. It scorns to tread in the footsteps of any predecessor, however illustrious.

It thirsts and burns for distinction; and if possible, it will have it, whether at the expense of emancipating slaves or enslaving freemen. Is it unreasonable, then, to expect that some man possessed of the loftiest genius, coupled with ambition sufficient to push it to its utmost stretch, will at some time spring up among us?"

Making political speeches was forbidden by the Lyceum, so Lincoln could not name him directly, but as Douglas was famous for his ambition, and newspaper articles both attacking and defending him had been widely read, he knew that his audience would understand to whom he was referring.

The Lyceum address was also calculated to make a strike at slavery, though Lincoln was careful in how he phrased these sentiments, not wishing to do what he had accused abolitionists of doing, that is, stirring up angry feelings in the crowd. But a large portion of his speech focused on what he called "the lawlessness of mobs"; a mob in

Alton, Illinois, had recently murdered a famous abolitionist by the name of Elijah P. Lovejoy and destroyed the printing presses with which he had printed abolitionist tracts. Lincoln's speech alluded to mobs that "threw printing presses into rivers"; the association could not have gone unnoticed. Lincoln declared that mob violence flew in the face of the laws that the previous generation, which had fought in the Revolutionary War for independence from England, had designed for the good of American society. Lincoln asserted that Americans had a duty to "swear by the blood of the Revolution never to violate in the least particular the laws of the country; and never to tolerate their violation by others." Just as his respect for the laws of the land prevented Lincoln from becoming a dyed in the wool abolitionist, demanding an end to slavery regardless of whether slave state voters consented or not, the same respect for the rule of law led Lincoln to demand that the rights of abolitionists to speak their mind not be interfered with.

Legislative Session of 1838

Partly as a result of vigorous campaigning by Lincoln, not only was he re-elected to the Illinois legislature, but John Todd Stuart narrowly beat Stephen A. Douglas in the race for the Congressional seat. Lincoln was nominated as the Whig candidate for Speaker of the House, but he lost by a few votes to the Democrat candidate, William L. D. Ewing, who had conceived a special resentment for Lincoln and the rest of the "Long Nine" for their part in getting Springfield named as the new Illinois capital.

The main issue before the legislature during this session was the public works program which had been voted into law while the debate over the new state capital was ongoing, and which was now running into funding difficulties owing to the financial crisis in 1837, and also to the fact that the state budget of Illinois had never really been large enough to make it work in the first place. The legislature was also debating whether to divide Sangamon County into several smaller counties, an issue which had been raised during the state capital debate, but which Lincoln had succeeded in tabling until the end of the previous legislative session.

Slavery was another issue that came before the Illinois assembly in 1838. Two resolutions supporting slavery were put forward: one condemning the governor of Maine for not extraditing men who had been charged with helping a slave escape his owners, and the other affirming that residents of non-slave states should not attempt to interfere with the property rights of slave owners from the southern states. Lincoln attempted to avoid having to make a stance on either issue by suggesting that the debates be postponed. However, in February of that year, yet another resolution related to slavery was proposed in the form of a resolution in which the Illinois legislature urged Congress not to end slavery in the District of Columbia.

Lincoln opposed this measure openly, and it was defeated when it came to a vote.

Election of President William Henry Harrison

In 1839, Lincoln campaigned on behalf of the Whig party's candidate for president of the United States, William Henry Harrison, who was considered a hero for his military service in the War of 1812, and in fighting Indians on the American frontier. Lincoln debated on Harrison's behalf against Democratic opponents during the fall and winter preceding the election. Harrison was running against the Democratic incumbent, Martin Van Buren, who had become unpopular due to the financial panic which had taken place during his administration. Lincoln's opponent during these debates were various prominent members of the Illinois Democratic party, including Stephen A. Douglas, who match wits with Lincoln on the subject of the Bank of the United States, which Lincoln supported. Douglas was in favor of the Van Buren proposal for an independent, that is, privatized sub-treasury, which Lincoln viewed as dangerous to the value of American currency. During these debates and speeches, spectators were impressed by the fact that Lincoln spoke without notes or reading his words from a prepared sheet of paper.

In the election of 1840 Lincoln ran for office again; this time he was subject to a nominating convention, which the Whigs had finally adopted in imitation of the Democrats. He did not expect that the party would choose to nominate him, and when they did so, he ascribed it to the fact they needed him to make speeches. Lincoln's preferred presidential candidate, Harrison, also won the 1840 election, defeating Martin Van Buren. Lincoln was elated at Harrison's election, but the Illinois legislature opened that year with strong feelings of partisan rancor. The state bank of Illinois, which was due to begin loan repayments which it could not afford at the end of the General Assembly's next legislative session, was particularly hated by the Democrats. If the bank could not make the payments, there was a chance it would fail, and so the Democrats, hoping to hasten this event, argued that the bank's loans should come due at the end of December, when the special session of the legislature ended. (The bank otherwise would not have to begin repayments until the end of the March, the closing date of the normal legislative session.)

When the issue came to a vote, Lincoln and his fellow Whigs saw that they would be out-voted. In order to prevent the vote from taking place, many Whigs stayed away from the church where the assembly was meeting, in the hopes that the remaining delegates would fail to constitute a quorum—that is, the minimum number of delegates legally required before a vote could take place. The Democrats, however, were sufficiently determined to have a vote that they managed to round up enough of their own members to constitute a quorum. Lincoln and the other Whigs present then attempted to leave the assembly chamber, but they found that the door was locked, and the other delegates refused to allow it to be unlocked. Undeterred, Lincoln broke a window and jumped out, followed by his fellow Whigs. When the sergeant at arms was commanded to run after Lincoln and bring him back by force, the sergeant protested that he couldn't possibly catch up with "Abe", because his legs were too long. This incident, which embarrassed Lincoln for years to come, was much laughed at by his Democratic opponents, and joking observances that Lincoln was "long-legged" and a "jumper" would follow him throughout his political career.

Lincoln's seven year stint of service in the Illinois General Assembly came to an end in March of 1841. He was, by this time, virtually unrecognizable as the skinny young man who had left working on the river boats wearing a pair of buckskin trousers that hung several inches above his socks. Newspaper articles were published encouraging the Whig party to nominate him to run for the office of governor of Illinois (Lincoln made a point of expressing his lack of interest in the position before it could be offered to him.) At the time, serving as governor was not seen the way it is seen today, as a gateway to wealth and even greater power in the future, but rather as a poorly paid four year interruption to the practice of one's career. Lincoln's lack of interest in being governor is therefore understandable, and not at all inconsistent with his ambition.

Some historians believe that Lincoln first began to conceive of a political career that would take him to Washington around this period in his life. He had achieved such standing in Illinois that, provided he continued to advance as rapidly as before, he was more or less bound to come to national prominence. However, he had not authored much legislation. Lincoln's contemporaries from this period of his life would be surprised when, as a more mature person,

Lincoln turned out to be a reformer, willing to gamble everything he had politically on ending slavery in his lifetime.

Romance and Courtships

In 1836, Lincoln courted, and eventually proposed marriage to, a woman by the name of Mary Owens, a cousin of his friend Mentor Graham. Owens was known to be highly intelligent, even intellectual, and well educated— far better educated than Lincoln himself. A voracious reader and a good conversationalist from a wealthy family, Owens first met Lincoln in 1833 on a visit to New Salem, and in 1836, acting on a matchmaking whim of her sister's, she returned to New Salem on the understanding that she and Lincoln would be spending time in each other's company with a view to becoming engaged later on.

Letters which Lincoln wrote to Owens would seem to indicate that he was deeply fond of her, but long after their courtship was over, Lincoln would say that he found Owens unattractive, because she had a matronly build and reminded him of his mother, and had proposed to her despite this because he considered himself honor bound to do so, and because he was afraid no other man would marry her. He was therefore shocked and embarrassed when he proposed to her and she turned him down. In a letter to a friend, he described himself as "mortified": "My vanity was deeply wounded by the reflection, that I had so long been too stupid to discover her intentions, and at the same time never doubting that I understood them perfectly; and also, that she whom I had taught myself to believe no body else would have, had actually rejected me with all my fancied greatness."

Owens' reasons for rejecting Lincoln seem to be related in part to his uncultivated upbringing. Owens told friends that although she knew Lincoln to be "good all the way through" she was convinced she could not be happy with him, because his knowledge of etiquette was poor. She seemed to find him deficient in chivalry. On one occasion, when they were crossing a creek in the company of other courting couples, Owens was miffed that Lincoln did not assist her in crossing the water, though all the other gentlemen present had done so for their companions. When she pointed this out to him, he replied that he thought she was smart enough to get across the water on her own. What Lincoln perceived as a compliment, Owens understood as an unforgivable lack of gallantry.

On another occasion, when Owens and Lincoln were out on a walk with the wife of Lincoln's friend, Bowling Green, Owens was unfavorably impressed by the fact that Lincoln did not offer to assist Mrs. Green in carrying her rather fat child when she showed signs of fatigue. Lincoln protested that he would happily have carried the child if Mrs. Green had asked him to do so, but Owens was troubled by the fact that he did not have the instinct to offer unasked. According to their friends, it was at this point that Owens declared that she did not think "Abe" would make a good husband. Their courtship began to decline from that point forward.

After Lincoln's relationship with Mary Owens came to an end, he declared that he thought he would be better off never marrying, and that he planned not to court anyone else. He said that other men "have been made fools of by the girls; but this can never be with truth said of me. I most emphatically, in this instance, made a fool of myself."

Mary Todd

In 1838, Lincoln first made the acquaintance of the woman he would later marry: Mary Todd. Like Mary Owens, she was a cousin of one of his male friends—in this case, his law partner, John Todd Stuart—and like Owens, she was well educated and a member of a wealthy Kentucky family. Todd was also short and plump, rather matronly, with a gift for biting sarcasm not unlike Lincoln's.

Lincoln's extraordinary intellect had never developed along lines that would recommend him in society; as garrulous and witty as he was when delivering speeches, he seemed to feel that his normal conversational style was not suited to polite society or mixed company, and as such, he often became quiet and tongue tied when attempting to converse with women. By contrast, Mary Todd was an accomplished socialite, capable of making intelligent, winning conversation with anyone who came into her orbit. According to observers, when Lincoln first met Todd, he sat and listened to her talk with a smile on his face, scarcely contributing anything to the conversation. This was during the winter of 1839-1840.

Todd seems to have considered Lincoln's chief recommendation to be his relationship with her cousin John Stuart Todd, whom she esteemed more highly than almost any other man; because they were so close, Todd believed that Lincoln and Stuart must be similar. Furthermore, by the time Lincoln and Todd met, Lincoln's star was well and truly on the rise, his reputation as a politician and a lawyer growing more famous by the day. These attributes may have made up for Lincoln's lack of family, lack of connections, poverty, and generally unpolished manner where Todd was concerned, but her family looked on Lincoln rather coolly, convinced that he and Mary would not get along.

Historian Michael Burlingame reports a social encounter between Lincoln and Todd that illustrates Lincoln's gaucheness.

"At a party in Jacksonville, Lincoln reportedly approached Mary Todd, saying: 'I want to dance with you in the worst way.' Afterwards she told him: 'Mr. Lincoln I think you have literally fulfilled your request – you have danced the worst way possible.'"

Todd had grown up in Lexington, Kentucky, the same state where Lincoln passed his childhood, but in a very different kind of world. Her parents were wealthy, and had sent her to a private boarding school where the students spoke only French. Her mother had died when she was six years old, and her father married very quickly after her death. Todd, and her brothers and sisters from their father's first marriage, were evidently very unhappy growing up under the care of their step mother. She was severe to her step children and indulgent toward the eight children she had with Todd's father. As soon as Elizabeth, the eldest of Mary Todd's sisters, was old enough, she married and moved to Springfield, where she was out of her step mother's grasp. Each of the younger sisters went to live with Elizabeth as soon as they were old enough, marrying and settling in Springfield themselves. All of them had little contact with their family in Lexington thereafter.

Lincoln was ten years older than Todd and an entire foot taller. Their personalities and dispositions were considered to be entirely opposite on another, even by Todd herself. Lincoln was careless about his personal appearance, and ignorant of how a formal household staffed by servants operated. After they were married, he often irritated Todd by answering a knock at the door himself instead of allowing a servant to do it, or by mishandling the silverware at meal times, or going about the house in his stocking feet without wearing slippers.

The courtship between Lincoln and Todd did not go entirely smoothly. In 1840, Lincoln, having supposedly fallen in love with another woman, came to the conclusion that he did not love Todd the way a man ought to love a woman he intended to marry. He wrote her a letter to this effect, which his friend Joshua Speed took from him and burned, telling Lincoln that he had a duty to break the engagement off in person.

Lincoln did so, and Todd wrote him a letter some time later declaring that he was free to court elsewhere if he wished to do so, but that her own feelings remained unchanged, and she would be open to renewing the engagement if he should change his mind.

Lincoln historian Michael Burlingame speculates that Lincoln might have begun to suspect that Todd suffered from a degree of psychological instability, and that she would need more emotional support from him than he could provide. While making an amateur medical diagnosis of figures from history is necessarily a speculative and imprecise practice, it seems self evident that there was some tendency towards mood disorders, at the least, in Mary Todd's family. A startlingly large number of Todd's numerous siblings—the men in particular—were noted for having violent tempers, a tendency toward sadism and cruelty, paranoia, and narcissistic self regard. Todd herself was described by her family as being "either in the attic or the garrett"—that is, either having an elevated mood or depressed spirits. This description has led some of Todd's biographers to diagnose her with bipolar disorder, or manic depression, as it was originally called.

In the years after Lincoln's assassination, during which her son Thomas, or Tad, died, Todd suffered paranoid delusions that her last surviving son, Robert, was deathly ill. Robert Lincoln felt compelled to have his mother committed to a mental institution after she became convinced that her house was on fire and attempted to jump through a window to escape the flames. After staying there for a time, she was released, and lived for the rest of her life with her sister Elizabeth Edwards in Springfield.

During the period when his engagement to Todd was broken, Lincoln dissolved his law partnership with John Todd Stuart, who, having finally been successful in his pursuit of a seat in Congress, was now spending most of his time in

Washington. Lincoln formed a new partnership with a man by the name of Stephen T. Logan, a renowned lawyer who had dissolved his own partnership with another lawyer over an ethical dispute. Logan was older than Lincoln, and was impressed with the younger man's abilities, having faced Lincoln in court and lost to him three times. Lincoln, whose study of the law was haphazard and self directed, learned a great deal from working with the more experienced lawyer. Lincoln and Logan worked together for three years and became good friends. During their partnership, Lincoln served as legal representation in a number of cases that appeared before the Illinois Supreme Court, which raised his prestige considerably.

During this period, Lincoln scarcely ever saw Mary Todd, a fact which depressed her somewhat. He attempted to court a sixteen year old girl named Sarah Butler, the daughter of his friend William Butler, at whose house he frequently took his meals. She refused him, however, probably because he was so much older than she; she declared that she looked on him more as an elder brother than a potential husband. Lincoln's conversations with his friends seemed to indicate that he had attempted to persuade himself that he was in love with Todd because he imagined her to be in love with him, and because of the money she would bring to the marriage. Nonetheless, he was tormented by his conscience in the belief that Todd was unhappy over their broken engagement. He wrote to his friend Joshua Speed that "it seems to me, I should have been entirely happy, but for the never absent idea, that there is one still unhappy whom I have contributed to make so. That still kills my soul. I can not but reproach myself, for even wishing to be happy while she is otherwise."

In September of 1841, Lincoln and Todd met again for the first time in more than a year, when Lincoln's friends, Mr. and Mrs. John Hardin, invited them both to the wedding of Hardin's sister. Burlingame describes their reunion thus:

"When the young people who were assembled at the Hardins' went for a ride, they left Mary behind because she had no escort. As she sadly watched their carriage depart, she was astonished to see Lincoln ride up. 'She went down & he said he had come for her to join the party.'"

Lincoln and Todd courted privately at the home of friends for a time, in order to reduce public gossip about their relationship, as it was not immediately certain how matters between them would proceed. During the period of their estrangement, Lincoln had been a source of counsel and advice to his friend Joshua Speed, who had ended up in a predicament not unlike Lincoln's: he had proposed to a woman after a short, whirlwind courtship, and afterwards suffered great anxiety that he had acted too hastily, and had only fooled himself into believing he loved her. Speed had, in the end, married the woman, whose name was Fanny, owing greatly to Lincoln's encouragement. Now that Lincoln was seeing Todd again, he consulted his friend for advice, asking him whether he found himself happy in his marriage to the woman he had entertained such grave doubts about. Speed assured him that his happiness in marriage was great, and that Lincoln should not delay any longer in getting married himself.

Abraham Lincoln and Mary Todd were married on November 4, 1842, making up their minds in the morning and celebrating the ceremony that night. They were married from the home of Todd's sister, Elizabeth Edwards, who reportedly was annoyed that Mary had not given her sufficient notice to bake a cake. The family was obliged to order refreshments for the ceremony from town, which arrived just before the wedding. They were married using the Episcopal marriage service, the formal, old fashioned language of which made several people in the wedding party break into laughter because of how poorly it seemed to suit the rough manners and humble attire of Lincoln, the backwoodsman.

Those who observed the Lincolns after the marriage rarely described them as seeming to be happy. A great many unflattering observations were made about Mary Todd Lincoln throughout her life as the wife of the President. At the White House, she was of course under constant observation. Many people declared that Mary and Abraham Lincoln were deeply unhappy, and much of the blame, historically, has been left at Mary's door. She was given to violent public displays when her mood was unsettled. She reportedly threw a cup of hot coffee at her husband the morning after they were married, while they were having breakfast at a tavern with other lodgers. Other stories depict her as smacking Lincoln on the nose with a stick of firewood after he ignored her request to draw up the fire.

There is some speculation that Todd and Lincoln may have been sexually intimate the night before their wedding. Some historians consider this a reasonable explanation for the haste with which they were married the next day, and the fact that their oldest son was born just barely nine months after the wedding day. There is no direct evidence of this either in letters or in the testimony of their friends, but the story seems to be compatible with the popular view that Lincoln felt honor bound to marry Todd and appeared anxious and unhappy on the day of his wedding.

It is worth noting that while Mary Todd Lincoln's temperament seemed to incline her toward public displays of temper and passion, Lincoln's notably reserved and controlled demeanor naturally disinclined him to conduct his private affairs where they could be observed. Mary Todd Lincoln may well have had emotional disturbances or psychological illnesses that contributed to the disharmony in her marriage, but what Lincoln may have said or done, either to provoke or exacerbate her, or else to make peace, no outsiders were in a position to observe. Therefore, his contributions to the marriage do not appear in the historical record. Additionally, nineteenth century prejudices regarding "female hysteria" make it virtually certain that Mary Todd Lincoln's real medical needs were overlooked and misunderstood. Lincoln has become such a beloved figure in American history that any unhappiness he may have felt during his marriage would almost inevitably be blamed on his wife, without due consideration for what role he might have played in his own marital unhappiness.

It is also worth noting that Mary's cousin John Todd Stuart gave Mary a great deal of credit for the illustrious political career that Lincoln had after his marriage. She was highly ambitious, which matched Lincoln's desires for his career, and Stuart was of the opinion that all Lincoln needed for real success was a "goad", which Mary provided. Her sister, Elizabeth Edwards, stated that, "Mrs. Lincoln was an ambitious woman – the most ambitious woman I ever saw – spurred up Mr. Lincoln, pushed him along and upward – made him struggle and seize his opportunities." It is doubtful whether Mary Todd Lincoln could have provided such incentive for Lincoln to "seize his opportunities" if she had a different sort of temperament. Perhaps Lincoln would not have run for president if not for the career that his wife's goading (as well as her wealth and social connections) made possible.

Speculation About Lincoln's Sexuality

Some historians and scholars believe it is possible that Abraham Lincoln experienced same-sex attraction and had sexual and romantic relationships with men at various times throughout his life. Naturally, this theory is controversial, and some historians reject it outright. However, in consideration of the fact that societal prejudice against homosexuality would have made it virtually impossible, until quite recently, for any scholar to seriously investigate this aspect of Lincoln's life, it is worth taking knee-jerk skepticism with a grain of salt.

The first biography of Lincoln was written by his close friend and law partner of more than twenty years, William Herndon, and it included a poem which Lincoln had written shortly after his sister's death in childbirth. The poem contained an allusion to a gay relationship between two men. Lincoln wrote the poem to mock his sister's in-laws, whom, as we discussed previously, he held responsible for her death, because they did not have a doctor present for the birth. Lincoln made the inference that his brother in law had sex with a man because he wished to insult him. But the indication that Lincoln was conscious of homosexuality when he was a very young man in interesting, as is the fact that Herndon included the poem in his biography—only for it to be deleted by subsequent editors of his work, until the 1980's.

Even more interesting is the assertion that Herndon himself was gay and that he and Lincoln were sexually and romantically intimate for some period of time, an assertion made by one of Herndon's living descendants. Due to Herndon's indisputably close relationship to Lincoln and the access he had to Lincoln's life, it would seem that if Lincoln were gay or bisexual, Herndon would be more likely than most people to know about it. However, if Herndon himself were gay, and particularly if he were in a relationship with Lincoln, his silence on that subject would make sense, as a matter of self-protection. Researcher Sylvia Rhue relates the following conversation about Herndon's family legacy:

"One day I was having lunch with Rev. Cindi Love, the executive director of Soulforce. I was telling her about my family history, my burgeoning love affair with Abraham Lincoln and my quest for more information. 'I have been researching Lincoln and found a lot about his relationships with men, and I am getting this from a many sources,' I told her. 'But I am puzzled about one thing: William Herndon has not mentioned or written anything that would indicate that Lincoln was gay.'

"She gave me a telling look and said, 'Well, here is the missing piece of your puzzle. My maiden name is Herndon. William Herndon was my great-great-uncle, and he was gay, and he was Lincoln's lover.' She went on to talk about how this information was handed down from generation to generation in the Herndon family."

While this is not conclusive evidence that Lincoln had romantic or sexual relationships with men, it presents an interesting possibility. As we have already discussed, Lincoln was decidedly awkward in his relationships with women, and he tended to prefer the company of other men in social situations. The difficulties in his marriage, though probably mostly attributable to Mary Todd Lincoln's poor mental health, might also have been exacerbated if Lincoln was conflicted about his sexuality.

The theory that Lincoln was gay or bisexual has other adherents as well. Psychologist C. A. Tripp, author of The Intimate World of Abraham Lincoln, was the first to widely publicize the theory of Lincoln's having had gay relationships. Additionally, famous gay writer and activist Larry Kramer claimed in 1999 to have uncovered portions of a long lost correspondence between Abraham Lincoln and his close friend Joshua Speed that contained unequivocal evidence of an affair between the two; scholars have claimed that these letters are almost certainly a forgery, but no definitive scientific analysis has yet been made.

In C. A. Tripp's book, historian Michael Chesson expresses this opinion in one of the afterwards:

"If Lincoln was a homosexual, or primarily so inclined, then suddenly our image of this mysterious man gains some clarity. Not everything falls into place. But many things do, including some important, even essential, elements of who Lincoln was, why he acted in the way he did, and a possible reason for his sadness, loneliness, and secretive nature."

There will likely never be complete certainty one way or the other regarding the secrets of Lincoln's sexuality, but the additional perspective provides an interesting reminder that homosexual relationships have always been a part of human history, though the role they played has often been censored and stricken from the historical record.

Chapter Four: The Congressman1843-1854

First Congressional Campaign

Lincoln's marriage to Mary Todd had one immediate effect on his career: she was strongly insistent that he run for Congress. Lincoln had been thinking somewhat along those lines himself, and in the winter of 1842-1843 he ran for Representative of Illinois' Seventh District. However, two of the men Lincoln was running against, John J. Hardin and Edward D. Baker, were personal friends of his, and when both of their campaigns began taking the lead over Lincoln's, he dropped out of the race and supported Baker, who was reckoned to be the best speaker and speech-maker in the Whig party after Lincoln.

However, Hardin (who was, incidentally, also a cousin of Mary Todd Lincoln) won by a single vote; afterwards, the Whig party of Illinois, partly at Lincoln's instigation, decided to nominate Edward D. Baker for the next term. The understanding was that Lincoln would then get the nomination after Baker. Ironically, Lincoln was told that one reason why he fell behind Baker in the race was because, since his marriage, he was considered to belong to the branch of the Whig party that was associated with aristocratic families and inherited wealth. Lincoln was deeply amused when he heard this, probably because it was so completely the reverse of the truth.

Henry Clay for President

In 1844, Henry Clay ran for president of the United States as the Whig candidate against Democrat James K. Polk. Henry Clay had long been the single man in politics that Lincoln admired more than any other—he referred to Clay as his "beau ideal" of a politician.

When Clay ran for president, Lincoln campaigned vigorously on his behalf, giving a number of speeches supporting the Whig agenda: support for the national bank, opposition to federal taxes, support for tariffs on foreign goods, and opposition to the annexation of Texas into the United States (his protest was on the grounds that Texas would enter the Union as a slave state). Lincoln gave speeches in support of Clay throughout Sangamon County, along with people such as Stephen T. Logan, his law partner. His principle opponent in these debates was the famous politician John Calhoun, who was running for Congress. However, despite Lincoln's efforts, Polk won the 1844 election, an even which Lincoln referred to as "as a great public calamity and a keen personal sorrow."

Law Partnership with William Herndon

Lincoln dissolved his law partnership with Stephen T. Logan after a few years when Logan's son was admitted to the bar and Logan expressed a wish to form a partnership with him. Lincoln, having twice been the junior partner in a law firm, decided this time to take on a younger lawyer as his partner. William Herndon was nine years Lincoln's junior and their partnership would last for the rest of Lincoln's life. (He was technically still Herndon's partner of record even while he was in Washington serving as President.) Herndon had been studying law in Lincoln and Logan's offices, and was, at the time Lincoln took him on as partner, in his own words, a "young, undisciplined, uneducated, wild man". Lincoln and Herndon first met because Herndon, an avowed Whig who hated slavery, was giving stump speeches supporting Lincoln's campaign for office. Lincoln introduced himself, and asked the young man if he should like to study law with him. Lincoln and Herndon were fast friends from that moment forward.

Lincoln's choice of Herndon as a partner baffled many of his friends at the time, as well as his later biographers, including Herndon himself. Some have speculated that he did it because Herndon had been disinherited by his cantankerous father for developing differing political views while away at college, including anti slavery views; Lincoln may have been reminded of his relationship with his own father, and taken Herndon on out of sympathy. Lincoln split all fees with Herndon equally, even in the earliest days of the partnership, before Herndon could realistically be said to have been pulling his own weight.

Lincoln's Election to Congress

Lincoln ran for Congress a second time in 1846; he initially faced opposition from John J. Hardin, despite the agreement that Lincoln would receive the nomination after Hardin and Baker's terms had ended. Lincoln had the support of a growing anti slavery movement which had started in certain Illinois counties, thanks to the work of an abolitionist named Benjamin Lundy. Lincoln rode a district circuit for his law practice that took him throughout the voting territories of the Seventh District, which was the district in which he was running, and this provided him with an opportunity to campaign while he practiced law. Lincoln was presented with the sum of two hundred dollars by the Whig party for his campaign expenses, but he only spent 75 cents of this money. Most of the expenses that political candidates at the time were put to was for alcohol, as political meetings were also social events at which the candidate was expected to provide refreshments. It is possible that Lincoln was not often called on to provide alcoholic refreshments, because he was himself an extremely moderate drinker and had often given speeches in support of the temperance movement.

Lincoln was insulted by the fact that Hardin was mounting a second campaign for Congress despite their previous agreement, but he refused to speak ill of Hardin in public or permit his supporters to do so on his behalf. This approach would characterize this phase of his political career. When Lincoln was a younger man, he was famed for his ability to use sarcasm to ridicule and tear down his opponents, but once his political career took him to the national level, he became famous instead for his astonishing patience and forbearance in the face of political attacks.

In February of 1846 Hardin withdrew from the race, and when the Whig nominating convention met in May, Lincoln received the nomination.

Lincoln's Democratic opponent in this election was Peter Cartwright, who spread rumors that Lincoln was not a religious man and that he was skeptical about Christianity. It was in fact the truth that never at any time in Lincoln's life had he been a regular churchgoer, but this seems to have been from social embarrassment over his country manners and poor clothing than from any lack of faith. Lincoln answered Cartwright's charges by declared that he had a deep belief in Scripture, his poor church attendance notwithstanding. In the end, Lincoln won the election, gathering 56% of the vote, a better showing than either Baker or Hardin had made in the previous two elections.

Mr. Lincoln Goes to Washington

Lincoln's sole term as a member of the House of Representatives constituted the entirety of his political career conducted at the national level prior to his returning to Washington as president in 1861. Lincoln's term in office was not uncommonly short by the standards of the day—it was fairly common for Representatives to serve one term and no more. Washington in the 1840's was not much more than a mid-sized town, populated mostly by politicians, who traveled to the nation's capital from around the country, usually leaving their wives behind. (The lack of women was blamed by European visitors for the lack of refinement in Washington's social scene.) The streets were muddy and livestock roamed about freely. It was fairly devoid of houses, businesses, and entertaining—politics was virtually the only thing that was done there.

Lincoln's time in the House of Representatives was similar in some respects to his first term in the Illinois General Assembly, in that he seemed content primarily to observe how things were done, rather than attempting to take an active part in authoring legislation and making speeches. He was reportedly very popular amongst his colleagues, who were charmed and entertained by his habit of telling humorous and (occasionally off color) stories. Lincoln was described by a journalist in Washington as a "universal favorite here – an entirely self-made man, and of singular and striking personal appearance." Speaker of the House Robert C. Winthrop, of Boston, remarked in later years that "for shrewdness, sagacity and keen, practical sense, he has had no superior in our day and generation." Nonetheless, he does not seem to have struck many of his colleagues as being a future candidate for higher office. Amos Tuck, one of the representatives from New Hampshire, thought well of Lincoln, but nonetheless could not seem to imagine him ever "taking high position in the country."

Speechmaking in the House of Representatives was difficult, because the Hall of House had been constructed in imitation of the Pantheon in

Rome, with a massive dome, and thus voices tended to be lost in the resounding echo. Lincoln, furthermore, as a junior member, had one of the worst seats in the Hall, in the very back row. Representatives who were giving speeches had to virtually shout to be heard, and even then not everyone bothered to listen. Historian Michael Burlingame writes that, "Tedium often prevailed in the House. Whenever a dull speaker took the floor, 'a forest of newspapers' appeared because members would not 'waste their time listening to his prosing.'" It was also not uncommon during this period for fights to break out amongst the members, who sometimes challenged each other to duels. It was a rough and colorful period in American politics, and Lincoln, the rangy frontiersman, was perhaps better suited to this "catch as catch can" atmosphere than he would have been to a more refined process of government.

The topic of the day, during the Thirtieth Congress, was the Mexican-American War, which had been opposed by the Whig party from its inception, and which was vigorously supported by James K. Polk, who had been elected president largely due to the war's popularity. Lincoln's boldest initiative during his Congressional career involved his staunch opposition to the war. Polk had justified the war by claiming that Mexican soldiers had crossed the border into the new state of Texas and killed Americans living there; the invasion of Mexico, which he authorized afterward, was therefore part of a defensive war. Lincoln, however, was skeptical; he authored a series of resolutions questioning Polk's assertion that the first assault against Americans happened on the American side of the border. He believed that the spot where Americans were attacked happened on Mexican soil, which made the American response a war of aggression, and he demanded that President Polk disclose the exact location of the first attack. (Polk ignored this demand.)

Because of this, Lincoln's legislation was referred to by a journalist as the "Spot Resolutions". Lincoln also voted for a resolution authored by another representative, which asserted that the war had been "unnecessarily and unconstitutionally begun" by Polk.

Lincoln's speech about the Mexican-American War was prompted, not only by his genuine political convictions, but by the fact that, as a freshman Congressman, he was eager to make his reputation and distinguish himself by making an excellent and memorable speech. This was a tradition amongst newcomers to the House, and the first speeches of first year representatives were listened to closely, so that his colleagues could discover whether he was likely to distinguish himself in politics. Lincoln's maiden speech was certainly memorable, but it elicited harsh consequences for him, both in the short term and later during his presidency. For instance, the following excerpt from his House speech was referred to frequently by southerners during the Civil War as a justification for secession:

"Any people anywhere, being inclined and having the power, have the right to rise up, and shake off the existing government, and for a new one that suits them better. This is a most valuable, – a most sacred right – a right, which we hope and believe, is to liberate the world. Nor is this right confined to cases in which the whole people of an existing government, may choose to exercise it. Any portion of such people that can, may revolutionize, and make their own, of so much of the territory as they inhabit. More than this, a majority of any portion of such people may revolutionize, putting down a minority, intermingled with, or near about them, who may oppose their movement."

The people to whom Lincoln was referring in this speech were the people of Texas, which had originally been a Mexican province, but was settled by a large number of Anglo (British descended) American colonists. Texas revolted against Mexican rule and declared itself an independent republic, which the government of Mexico did not formally recognize. When Texas chose to join the United States, however, the Mexican government attempted to reclaim the territory, leading to the outbreak of the war.

Lincoln's speech closely reflected the views of his political party. Many of his fellow Whigs, including sympathetic journalists writing in newspapers, declared that his speech placed him amongst the best and ablest speakers in the House. Democrats, however, were (perhaps understandably) infuriated by the content of the speech and the charges he made against Polk. For Lincoln, the most disastrous reaction to the speech came from his former supporters in

Illinois. Democratic Congressmen accused Lincoln of hiding his views about the war from his constituents until after he was elected. (Lincoln must have suffered somewhat in comparison with his former opponent John J. Hardin, who, after losing the Congressional race to Lincoln, volunteered to fight in the war and was later killed in battle.)

The Mexican-American War was popular in Illinois, and Lincoln's speech was not taken kindly by those who had fought in it, or sent friends and family to fight or die in it. He was declared "the Benedict Arnold" of his home district by a gathering of angry voters in Sangamon County. (Benedict Arnold was an American general who defected to the British side in the middle of the Revolutionary War.) Even some Whig newspapers declared that Lincoln had "put the interests of [his] party above those of the country," although none directly criticized his stance on the war.

None of these reactions seems to have come as much of a surprise to Lincoln, but he was a bit taken aback when William Herndon echoed the general Illinois opposition to Lincoln's criticism of Polk and the war. Lincoln wrote to Herndon in reply that if he had been in Congress, and if he had learned the things Lincoln had learned, he would have acted as Lincoln acted. Herndon was compelled to advise Lincoln that his views on the war had made him anathema back in Illinois, and that if he should run for another term, he certainly would not be elected. This was in spite of the fact that some Whigs were openly encouraging Lincoln to run again, even though it was by now traditional for Whig party leaders to only serve one term. Lincoln was pleased to hear of this; he liked the idea of serving another term. However, Stephen T. Logan received the nomination instead. (Logan would lose the election to his Democratic opponent.) Lincoln's term in the House of Representatives came to an end in 1849.

Lincoln's Resolution to Abolish Slavery in the District of Columbia

Before Lincoln left office and returned to Illinois, he authored a resolution calling for an end to slavery in the District of Columbia. Debates over slavery fairly dominated Congress in 1848, and while Whigs were often hesitant to give full throated opposition to slavery for fear of alienating potential political allies, certain members of Congress brought forth a number of different resolutions touching on the topic of slavery, all of which met with intense debate. There were resolutions attempting to introduce slavery into western territories such as Oregon, California, and New Mexico; when these measures were defeated, it was declared "the only signal defeat the slave power has ever experienced under this government."

In Washington, Lincoln was exposed to slavery first hand and at close quarters. Walking through the city, Lincoln had to pass by an open pen, similar to a corral for livestock, which held slaves of all ages and sex crammed together, awaiting sale at auction. Such sights turned his stomach. Furthermore, he was learning more about how the slave trade operated, its economic significance, and the attitudes of the southern states toward what was termed the "peculiar institution". After voting to table a resolution that called for an end to slave trading in the District of Columbia, Lincoln announced that he had done so because he intended to offer another resolution in its place, calling for the complete abolition of slavery in the District—for, as Lincoln said, there was no point in slavery being legal at all if the trading of slaves was illegal.

The contents of Lincoln's resolution reflected his longstanding belief that the only practical way to eliminate slavery was to do so in a way that reflected an understanding of the economic investment that slave owners had made in their ownership of human beings. He proposed tha, starting from a certain date, children born to slave mothers in the District of Columbia should be born free, and that the owners of their mothers should be responsible for the children's education. In return, the children would work for the owners as apprentices to some kind of skilled trade until they came of age, at which point they would be free men. Lincoln also proposed compensating any slave owners who agreed to emancipate their slaves immediately. To mollify Congressman on both sides of the slavery question who did not want a large number of free blacks hanging around in their city, the resolution further stated that fugitive slaves who came to Washington would be returned to their owners, and that any free black man who wanted to emigrate to another country would be given money to do so. The resolution, if it passed the House, would come before the ordinary voters of Washington for ratification. This reflected Lincoln's conviction that slavery could only be ended Constitutionally, by the consent of the people.

The reaction to Lincoln's resolution was typical: southerners called him an abolitionist, abolitionists declared that he was practically a supporter of slavery. Though the resolution did not pass, it was the first sign of the reformer Lincoln would be when he was president. One of his colleagues in Congress said of him that "he is a strong but judicious enemy to Slavery, and his efforts are usually very practical, if not always successful."

Return to Law Practice

"Discourage litigation. Persuade your neighbors to compromise whenever you can. Point out to them how the nominal winner is often a real loser—in fees, expenses, and waste of time. As a peacemaker the lawyer has a superior opportunity of being a good man."

Abraham Lincoln, "Notes for a Law Lecture"

Lincoln returned from the bustling capital of the nation to his law office in Springfield, Illinois, in 1849. His offices were dreary and the cases he had to try were less interesting to him than they had been formerly. Thanks to the completion of the Illinois and Michigan Canal, and the establishment of railroads and telegraph lines, most of the cases which came before the lawyers of Springfield in the 1850's were now commercial cases between businesses, rather than personal matters between the people of Springfield and the Eighth Circuit, an area larger than the entire state of Rhode Island, which

Lincoln continued to ride. Lincoln preferred the traditional role of the lawyer as a peacemaker in feuds between neighbors, and would not take a client's case if he felt that they were only legally but not morally in the right.

Lincoln was also known to charge notoriously low fees for his legal services. His fellow lawyers in the district found his cheap prices annoying, because they drove down the fees everyone else was able to collect. Lincoln felt strongly that it was unjust to charge everyone who walked through his door offering to pay, or to always charge them as much as they were willing to pay. He wrote:

"[The] matter of fees is important, far beyond the mere question of bread and butter involved. Properly attended to, fuller justice is done to both lawyer and client. An exorbitant fee should never be claimed. As a general rule never take your whole fee in advance, nor any more than a small retainer. When fully paid beforehand, you are more than a common mortal if you can feel the same interest in the case as if something were still in prospect for you, as well as for your client. And when you lack interest in the case the job will very likely lack skill and diligence in the performance. Settle the amount of fee and take a note in advance. Then you will feel that you are working for something, and you are sure to do your work faithfully and well. Never sell a fee note – at least not before the consideration service is performed. It leads to negligence by losing interest in the case, and dishonesty in refusing to refund when you have allowed the consideration to fail."

Death of Edward Lincoln

Edward, or Eddy, as his parents called him, was the second child of Abraham and Mary Todd

Lincoln. He died a few months before his fourth birthday, in 1850. Historian Michael Burlingame believes that Eddy's death, which affected Lincoln profoundly, might have been the catalyzing event which deepened Lincoln's moral thinking, shaping the stance he would adopt when he returned to politics. Lincoln's biographers note that the Lincoln who served in the Illinois General Assembly and the House of Representatives was markedly different from the Lincoln who helped found the Illinois Republican Party, participated in the famous Lincoln vs. Douglas debates, and became president. Lincoln's focus as a younger man had been to distinguish himself by making good speeches and winning as much advantage for his political party as he could. But by the time he returned to politics, he was focused on the issues that would shape the nation's destiny.

A long poem, written as an elegy on Eddy's death, was printed in the Illinois State Journal shortly after he was buried. The first stanza is reproduced below:

> Those midnight stars are sadly dimmed,
>
> That late so brilliantly shone,
>
> And the crimson tinge from cheek and lip,
>
> With the heart's warm life has flown –
>
> The angel of Death was hovering nigh,
>
> And the lovely boy was called to die.

When he returned to politics, Lincoln would no longer ridicule his opponents or write anonymous satirical newspaper essays about them. His mind would be set on higher matters.

The Kansas-Nebraska Act

In 1854, the Missouri Compromise, which stipulated that slavery could not exist north of the Mason Dixon Line, was, in effect, overturned by the Kansas-Nebraska Act. The Kansas-Nebraska Act was presented to Congress by Lincoln's old opponent, Stephen A. Douglas, and its passage introduced the concept of "popular sovereignty"—the idea that, in states where slavery had been made illegal by the Missouri Compromise, voters should be permitted to decide whether to allow slavery or not. The Kansas-Nebraska Act shocked and outraged the residents of the free states, and even those who had been lukewarm on the issue of slavery before were suddenly stirred to action. The gulf between those who supported slavery and those who opposed it widened to an uncrossable breach, and the lines along which the country would be divided during the Civil War a decade later began to be marked out.

Lincoln was inspired to return to politics, running for a seat in the Senate in the 1854 election. At the time, senators were selected by the vote of the Illinois legislature, rather than by the vote of the people. Though Lincoln gained a great deal of support at the beginning of his campaign, he gradually began to fall behind other candidates, and eventually asked his supporters to switch their support to the candidate of his choice, Lyman Trumbull.

Lincoln's Peoria Speech

On October 16, 1854, shortly before his run for Senate, Stephen A. Douglas gave a speech defending his role in the Kansas-Nebraska Act before a large audience in Peoria, Illinois. It was arranged that Lincoln would also be there, and that when Douglas had finished speaking, Lincoln would give a speech in response. The speech which Lincoln gave constituted the most eloquent expression of anti-slavery sentiment so far in his career, and it raised Lincoln's national profile considerably, establishing him as one of the pre-eminent men in Illinois politics. In the following extract from the speech, Lincoln refers to the view that the framers of the Constitution took with regards to slavery:

"I particularly object to the new position which the avowed principle of this Nebraska law gives to slavery in the body politic. I object to it because it assumes that there can be moral right in the enslaving of one man by another. I object to it as a dangerous dalliance for a few free people—a sad evidence that, feeling prosperity we forget right—that liberty, as a principle, we have ceased to revere. I object to it because the fathers of the republic eschewed, and rejected it. The argument of "Necessity" was the only argument they ever admitted in favor of slavery; and so far, and so far only as it carried them, did they ever go. They found the institution existing among us, which they could not help; and they cast blame upon the British King for having permitted its introduction. Before the constitution, they prohibited its introduction into the north-western Territory—the only country we owned, then free from it. At the framing and adoption of the constitution, they forbore to so much as mention the word "slave" or "slavery" in the whole instrument. In the provision for the recovery of fugitives, the slave is spoken of as a "person held to service or labor" [...] These are the only provisions alluding to slavery. Thus, the thing is hid away, in the constitution, just as an afflicted man hides away a wen or a cancer, which he dares not cut out at once, lest he bleed to death; with the promise, nevertheless, that the cutting may begin at the end of a given time."

In this portion of the speech, Lincoln argues that, far from slavery being an American institution, it was a messy problem that the country's founders had attempted to distance themselves from, and which they would have abolished if not for what he calls "necessity". In other words, Lincoln argues that the Revolutionary generation never intended for slavery to spread beyond the states where it existed at the time America was founded in 1789. The Kansas-Nebraska Act, therefore, violated the spirit of the Constitution. Once again, Lincoln's arguments against slavery were based in his interpretation of the law of the land. His personal, moral repugnance for slavery, however keenly felt, did not, in his mind, constitute an adequate legal or political argument for overthrowing it.

Chapter Five: The Road to the Presidency 1855-1860

Founding of the Republican Party

The Kansas-Nebraska Act forced a rearrangement of the existing political parties. Whigs were divided along pro and anti slavery lines, as were Democrats, and there were other parties, such as the Liberty and Free Soil parties, which were drawn into alignment with the majority parties during the re-organization process. Lincoln was instrumental in forming the Republican party in Illinois by drawing together all those who opposed slavery into a single anti slavery party.

Lincoln continued to position himself as something other than an abolitionist; in a letter to his friend Joshua Speed, he declared, "I only oppose the extension of slavery." It would perhaps be more accurate to say that, as a *politician*, he only opposed slavery's extension; as a *person*, he would only be too happy if slavery vanished from the earth. He remained committed to attempts to eradicate the "peculiar institution" by legal means, while acknowledging the financial difficulties the southerners would incur. But he had seen such attempts at gradually ending slavery, with compensation for the slave owners, fail before; Henry Clay had attempted it in Kentucky, with no success. Lincoln declared that the "Autocrat of all the Russias will resign his crown, and proclaim his subjects free republicans sooner than will our American masters voluntarily give up their slaves."

There were some difficulties in attempting to unite all anti-slavery voters in a single party because of the degree to which anti-slavery was linked with other controversial political doctrines. Many prohibitionists were anti-slavery, though prohibition was anything but universally popular. Nativists, who opposed Catholics and all who were not American born, tended to be anti-slavery as well. But respectable former Whigs would not consider aligning themselves with such prejudiced minority views, even to consolidate opposition to slavery.

Lincoln had said that he was opposed only to the spread of slavery, rather than slavery itself, and he proved it by campaigning for a restoration of the Missouri Compromise and an end to popular sovereignty. Kansas was still a territory, rather than a state; if popular sovereignty were not overturned, Lincoln declared, he would oppose statehood for Kansas. Lincoln also made a career out of giving speeches wherever Douglas gave them. Any time Douglas attempted to defend the Kansas-Nebraska Act, Lincoln was present to answer him. Over time, the popularity of the nativists and the prohibitionists declined, and anti-slavery became a unifying cause in itself.

The first official meeting of the new Republican Party was in Wisconsin, but Republicanism quickly spread throughout the free northern states. The first Republican National Convention was held in Philadelphia on June 19, 1856, where it nominated a former California senator named John Fremont as its first candidate for president. Lincoln was considered for vice-president, but did not receive the nomination. However, he came in second of the fifteen vice presidential candidates.

The Lincoln vs. Douglas Debates

By the late 1850's, Douglas, author of the Kansas-Nebraska Act, was no longer a supporter of President James Buchanan, though he had supported him strongly during his presidential campaign and been instrumental in helping him get elected. Their ideological division arose over the issue of popular sovereignty—the belief that voters in new American states and territories should be allowed to decide whether slavery should become legal in those regions.

Douglas's seeming defection from the mainstream Democratic party resulted in a massive shake up of the political status quo of the day; moderate Democrats flocked to Douglas's standard, and even some Republicans were inclined to support him as the lesser of two evils. It was well known that Douglas wanted to run for president, and it had always been assumed that he would run as a Democrat. However, the Democratic party had suffered a decline in general popularity due to the controversy over the Kansas-Nebraska Act; rumor began to spread that perhaps Douglas would join, and run as a member of, the newly formed Republican party. As Douglas was the incumbent for the Illinois senate seat, and as Lincoln was well known to be the favored Republican candidate for the next election, Lincoln was rather annoyed by Republican party leaders making much of Douglas.

Douglas was an extremely popular public speaker. Nicknamed "the Little Giant" for the gravity of his bearing (and the shortness of his stature), Douglas had the polished bearing and classical education that Lincoln lacked. He was also famous throughout the country, unlike Lincoln, who was little known outside of Illinois at this time. Lincoln and Douglas had known each other since they were both young men, and Lincoln had a certain amount of respect for Douglas's ambitions and accomplishments, but he did not respect Douglas's political agenda. Lincoln considered Douglas a demagogue—that is, a politician who gains popular support by appealing to people's fears, prejudices, and emotions rather presenting them with logical explanations and arguments for his policies. Douglas would lie unscrupulously just to provoke an emotional reaction from his audience. Lincoln preferred to break down the pros and cons of an issue in simple language his audience could understand and then explain why he preferred the one side over the other.

In the end, Douglas did not switch his membership to the Republican party. In fact, he claimed that he never had any intention of doing so, which was a deliberate fabrication, because he had entertained Republican leaders while he was still in Washington, and told them that he was no longer a friend to the south, or to slavery. When Douglas returned to Illinois in 1858 to defend his senate seat, it was as a Democrat; as expected, his opponent was Lincoln, the Republican nominee.

Lincoln and Douglas were both accomplished public speakers, but Douglas's reputation was huge; he was a superstar of his day. Lincoln was barely known, by comparison. But as they were both running for senate in Illinois, Lincoln made the proposal that he and Douglas should speak jointly, so that the voters of Illinois could form an impression of them as candidates and better understand the differences in their platforms.

Douglas was not enthusiastic about this proposition. In public, he said that he was inclined to refuse Lincoln's request, because he was so famous, and Lincoln so little known, that the advantage must flow all one way—that is, Lincoln would benefit from being seen by the same crowds that had gathered to see Douglas, while Douglas could scarcely benefit from being associated with Lincoln in any way. There was also the fact that Douglas knew perfectly well that, obscure though he was, Lincoln was an impressive debater, and the outcome of a public speaking contest between them was by no means guaranteed to be in Douglas's favor. As Douglas observed to a friend,

"I do not feel, between you and me, that I want to go into this debate. The whole country knows me and has me measured. Lincoln, as regards myself, is comparatively unknown, and if he gets the best of this debate, and I want to say he is the ablest man the Republicans have got, I shall lose everything and Lincoln will gain everything. Should I win, I shall gain but little."

Nonetheless, once Lincoln had issued the challenge, Douglas could not turn him down without looking like a coward. Indeed, the terms on which Douglas finally accepted him were considered somewhat cowardly, at least by the pro Republican newspapers: he agreed to debate Lincoln once in each of the nine voting districts in Illinois, excluding Springfield and Chicago, because they had both already given speeches there. Douglas drew up an itinerary, naming each of the cities in which he would consent to debate with Lincoln, and the dates on which the debates should take place. He also proposed a format for the debates. They would last for three hours: the speaker who opened would have an hour, the speaker who replied to them would speak for an hour and a half, and the first speaker would have half an hour to reply to the second speaker. Douglas, cheekily, proposed that they alternate the first speaker slots, but in such a way a way that he was given four of the opening speaker slots while Lincoln was given three. Lincoln made a token protest, but ultimately agreed to the schedule Douglas proposed.

The Republican newspapers considered Douglas cowardly for agreeing to a mere seven debates and suggested that Douglas was afraid to face to Lincoln in a public contest. The Democratic newspapers considered it laughable to suppose that a person with Douglas's reputation could be frightened of "a Mr. A. Lincoln".

The debates began in Ottawa, Illinois, on August 21, 1858. The topic of the debates was slavery. Slavery was the single most hotly contested issue in the United States in 1858, and because of his association with popular sovereignty and the Nebraska-Delaware Act, Stephen A. Douglas was the face of it. Douglas was not a pleasant opponent to debate; he had a pompous air, a superfluity of words, and he seemed to feel no scruple at lying outright about his opponents or the issues in order to stir up feeling. Lincoln, on the other hand, had a reputation for honesty, an obvious and sincere belief in the anti slavery platform, and a kind of modest, unassuming likeability that Douglas manifestly lacked. The two debaters seemed evenly matched at the outset of their campaigns for the Senate.

The main thrust of Douglas's platform seemed to be convincing his audiences that a vote for Lincoln was a vote for abolition, racial equality, citizenship for free blacks, and every nightmare that sheltered white imaginations could conjure up with respect to a fully bi-racial society. He argued for the inherent inferiority of black people a face stemming back to the creation of the world, ordained by God. The truth of the matter is that if Lincoln had believed in any of these things, he would have been at the forefront of the radical abolitionists; but in fact, the radical abolitionists considered Lincoln's stance on slavery to be so backwards that there was scarcely any difference between him and Douglas.

When it came Lincoln's turn to speak at the first debate, he answered Douglas's assertions about his opinions on slavery thus:

"I have no purpose directly or indirectly to interfere with the institution of slavery in the States where it exists. I believe I have no lawful right to do so, and I have no inclination to do so. I have no purpose to introduce political and social equality between the white and black races. There is a physical difference between the two, which in my judgment will probably forever forbid their living together upon the footing of perfect equality, and inasmuch as it becomes a necessity that there must be a difference, I, as well as Judge Douglas, am in favor of the race to which I belong, having the superior position. I have never said anything to the contrary, but I hold that notwithstanding all this, there is no reason in the world why the negro is not entitled to all the natural rights enumerated in the Declaration of Independence, the right to life, liberty, and the pursuit of happiness. [Applause, loud cheers.] I hold that he is as much entitled to these as the white man. I agree with Judge Douglas that he is not my equal in many respects – certainly not in color, perhaps not in moral or intellectual endowment. But in the right to eat the bread, without the leave of anybody else, which his own hand earns, he is my equal and the equal of Judge Douglas and the equal of every living man."

In this speech, Lincoln reveals the consistency of his opinion on slavery—his lack of belief in racial equality, his feeling that it was necessary for slavery to be ended only by those with the "legal right" to do so, and his belief that blacks had as much right to life, liberty, and the pursuit of happiness as whites. It was, in short, not a wide eyed reformer's dream of improbable social harmony, as Douglas attempted to make it sound, but a summary of what would turn out to be a successful political strategy to end the institution of slavery in the United States.

Opinion was naturally divided regarding who had won the first of the Lincoln – Douglas debates; the Republican newspapers reported a victory for Lincoln, and the Democratic papers, naturally, reported that Douglas had carried the day. Transcripts of the debate were printed in all the newspapers, with the Democratic papers correcting and editing the stenographer's mistakes in Douglas's speeches and leaving the Lincoln speech in the rough state in which it was scribbled down—and the Republican papers returned the favor, polishing up Lincoln's transcripts and leaving Douglas's in an unedited state. The Chicago Times even went so far as to strip out large portions of Lincoln's speech so as to make him sound like a weak, confused speaker.

The debates carried on from August to October of 1858, when the Senatorial election was held. Lincoln, in one of those peculiar outcomes that are seemingly unique to American politics, won the popular vote in Illinois, but because Senators were technically selected by the legislature and not the people, Douglas was elected by the General Assembly. However, the debates had forever altered the course of Lincoln's career. He had become genuinely famous on a national level. Lincoln's own sense of justice to himself made him feel that he had been the real winner of the debates, despite the fact that they had resulted in Douglas's being elected. He collected and edited the text of his speeches and published them as a book, which became an instant best-seller. The Republican party took Lincoln's debates as a textbook of party policy on the subject of slavery. In short, by participating in the debates and publishing the book of his speeches, Lincoln "had created for himself a national reputation that [was] both envied and deserved."

Lincoln was now sufficiently famous throughout the country to be considered a viable candidate for his party's nomination to run for president, and indeed, in 1860, the Republican nomination lighted on him. As a journalist in the *Peoria Message* wrote in 1858, "Defeat works wonders with some men. It has made a hero of Abraham Lincoln."

Cooper Union Speech

In 1859, Lincoln was invited, largely on the strength of his performance in the debates against Douglas, to give a speech at the church where Henry Ward Beecher was a clergyman. Beecher, brother of the novelist Harriet Beecher Stowe whose anti slavery novel *Uncle Tom's Cabin* was one of the most widely read books of its time, was himself a famous abolitionist. His church was located in Brooklyn, in New York city, which goes to show just how wide ranging Lincoln's reputation had become by this time.

The occasion of Lincoln accepting Beecher's invitation is only remarkable because it was the occasion of Lincoln giving one of the most extraordinary speeches of his career. He had chosen to address a statement which Douglas had made during one of his debate speeches, in which he asserted that the founders of the United States "when they framed the Government under which we live, understood this question [slavery] just as well, and even better, than we do now." Lincoln chose to spend months exhaustively researching where each individual framer of the Constitution stood with respect to the few specific provisions the Constitution makes regarding slavery, in order to discern precisely what was intended by the founders regarding the federal government's control over slavery.

The venue for the speech had to be moved from Beecher's church to a larger location called the Cooper Institute when more than 1500 people showed up to hear Lincoln. The following is a long excerpt from the speech Lincoln gave during what many consider to have been his finest hour as an orator:

"When you make these declarations, you have a specific and well-understood allusion to an assumed Constitutional right of yours, to take slaves into the federal territories, and to hold them there as property. But no such right is specifically written in the Constitution. That instrument is literally silent about any such right. We, on the contrary, deny that such a right has any existence in the Constitution, even by implication.

"Your purpose, then, plainly stated, is that you will destroy the Government, unless you be allowed to construe and enforce the Constitution as you please, on all points in dispute between you and us. You will rule or ruin in all events.

"This, plainly stated, is your language. Perhaps you will say the Supreme Court has decided the disputed Constitutional question in your favor. Not quite so. But waiving the lawyer's distinction between dictum and decision, the Court have decided the question for you in a sort of way. The Court have substantially said, it is your Constitutional right to take slaves into the federal territories, and to hold them there as property. When I say the decision was made in a sort of way, I mean it was made in a divided Court, by a bare majority of the Judges, and they not quite agreeing with one another in the reasons for making it; that it is so made as that its avowed supporters disagree with one another about its meaning, and that it was mainly based upon a mistaken statement of fact - the statement in the opinion that "the right of property in a slave is distinctly and expressly affirmed in the Constitution."

"An inspection of the Constitution will show that the right of property in a slave is not *"distinctly* and *expressly* affirmed" in it. Bear in mind, the Judges do not pledge their judicial opinion that such right is *impliedly* affirmed in the Constitution; but they pledge their veracity that it is *"distinctly* and *expressly"* affirmed there - "distinctly," that is, not mingled with anything else - "expressly," that is, in words meaning just that, without the aid of any inference, and susceptible of no other meaning.

"If they had only pledged their judicial opinion that such right is affirmed in the instrument by implication, it would be open to others to show that neither the word "slave" nor "slavery" is to be found in the Constitution, nor the word "property" even, in any connection with language alluding to the things slave, or slavery; and that wherever in that instrument the slave is alluded to, he is called a "person;" - and wherever his master's legal right in relation to him is alluded to, it is spoken of as "service or labor which may be due," - as a debt payable in service or labor. Also, it would be open to show, by contemporaneous history, that this mode of alluding to slaves and slavery, instead of speaking of them, was employed on purpose to exclude from the Constitution the idea that there could be property in man."

It is not uncommon in the twenty first century for a political speaker to present a speech that has been deeply researched and makes reference to obscure historical facts, but it was a sign of deep erudition in a speaker of the nineteenth century to display such mastery and interpretation of historical fact. Lincoln's ability, here demonstrated, to delve deep into the Constitution and come to an independent understanding of what it signifies and what sort of effect its framers intended it to have on the governments of future generations, made him a demonstrably fit candidate for the presidency. Even those who little understood such matters themselves could see that Lincoln, whether or not they agreed with him on the issues, had thought deeply about them, and had the greatest respect for the nation's founding documents.

Nomination

By the conclusion of the debates with Stephen A. Douglas, Lincoln had started to think seriously about his chances of becoming president. At first, he did not think it was very likely he could succeed. When friends urged him to pursue the nomination, and declared that he was the first and ablest Republican of the day, more electable than any other well known man of his party, Lincoln professed himself flattered, and said that he should like to be president, but that he was convinced that "there is no such good luck in store of me as the presidency."

The principle thing which made Lincoln suitable for receiving his party's nomination was the fact that he was a moderate: neither a pro slavery advocate for popular sovereignty, nor a radical abolitionist demanding and immediate end to slavery whether the south agreed or not. Slavery was the defining issue of the election of 1860, and Lincoln seemed to represent an electable compromise between the worst fears of the south and the worst fears of the north.

Lincoln campaigned for his nomination in a modest way, giving speeches where he was able. From sheer financial necessity he returned to his law practice, which limited the amount of time he was able to spend giving stump speeches. He faced opposition from more than his own modesty; the Republicans fielded a number of qualified candidates in the 1860 election, many of them more qualified, in Lincoln's opinion, than himself. These included many of the men Lincoln would hire onto his own cabinet once he became president, such as William H. Seward, the Senator from New York.

Lincoln was considered to have, at most, an outside chance of getting the nomination. That his name had been put forth at all was considered to have been a mere courtesy nod to the fact that he had risen to such prominence in recent years. However, Lincoln had a circle of exceedingly loyal friends in Springfield, men who knew his abilities well and were convinced that he was the man of the hour. Lincoln had a remarkable ability to foster deep trust among his comrades, and it seemed that anyone who knew him well became exceptionally loyal to him. Said one of Lincoln's supporters at the second Republican National Convention of 1860, "this Convention is literally sitting on a volcano of its own enthusiasm for Abraham Lincoln, and just aching to give three cheers and a tiger for Old Abe". Enthusiasm for Lincoln the candidate was spreading throughout the party, and where it was slow to spread, Lincoln's partisans were on the spot to fan the flames.

The strategy of Lincoln's friends was to make him the second choice of those who would not adopt him as their first. In this way, when supporters of Seward, Chase, Bates, etc., came into conflict—and all of them had alienated various other factions of the Republican party—they discovered that they could, at least, all agree on Lincoln. The fact that Lincoln was a frontiersman of the American west was also a point strongly in his favor—the western frontier was where the great issues of the day were centered, and it was thought that if the Republican candidate came from the west, more westerners would be likely to vote for him.

The night before the convention selected their nominee, Seward's supporters were so confident of their victory that they consumed more than three hundred bottles of champagne. They were to be disappointed, however, as well as hung over. Thanks to clever and indefatigable lobbying on the part of Lincoln's supporters, and to the strategy of making him the ideal compromise candidate, his nomination was secured. One of his supporters described the scene at the convention when Lincoln's name was called: "the uproar that followed was beyond description. Imagine all the hogs ever slaughtered in Cincinnati giving their death squeals together, a score of big steam whistles going together...and you can conceive something of the same nature." Five thousand people, men and women, screamed at the top of their lungs for five minutes. This demonstrated to the delegates the extent of Lincoln's popular support, and instructed them how they ought to vote.

When enough state's delegates had cast their votes for Lincoln, a telegram was dispatched to the offices of the *Illinois State Journal*, where Lincoln and a group of his supporters were anxiously awaiting the news. Reportedly, after reading the telegram containing the news of his nomination, Lincoln thanked his supporters, then announced, "I must go home; there is a little short woman there that is more interested in this matter than I am." In truth, Mary Todd Lincoln was keenly invested in her husband's political career, and she had told more than one person that she was "determined" to make him president.

Election

The presidential election of 1860 had a great riding on it. Prominent slave states, including South Carolina, Mississippi, and Alabama, had already announced that if an anti slavery candidate was elected president, they would hold conventions to determine what their response would be—in other words, to determine whether they were prepared to secede from the Union. Seven states would, in fact, secede prior to Lincoln's inauguration.

Lincoln's election was virtually guaranteed by virtue of the fact that Stephen A. Douglas had split the Democratic party along north – south lines by his support for popular sovereignty. The divide ran so deeply that during the Democratic convention in Charleston, a faction of virulently pro slavery southern Democrats walked out—this included all the delegates from Alabama, Florida, Georgia, Louisiana, Mississippi, South Carolina, Texas, most of the Arkansas delegates, and one of the delegates from Delaware. The Southern Democrats ended up forming their own party and putting forward their own candidate in the race, John C. Breckenridge of Kentucky, former vice president under James Buchanan. The remnants of the mainstream Democratic party supported the candidacy of Stephen A. Douglas of Illinois, Lincoln's old debating opponent. A fourth candidate, John Bell, ran as the candidate for the Constitutional Union party.

Voter turnout at the 1860 election was the highest in American history to that point. The divisions in the country that would short erupt as the fault lines of the Civil War meant that almost all of the candidates received votes from their own part of the country and nowhere else. Lincoln received not one electoral vote from the south, and Breckinridge and Bell did not receive any from the north or the west. For Lincoln, in the southern states that soon formed the Confederacy, not a single ballot was cast. The fact that Lincoln was elected despite the overwhelming lack of support of southern voters was cited by secessionists as a justification for leaving the Union; they held that if the south were to be ruled by Lincoln's administration, it would be tantamount to governing without the consent of the governed.

With these bitter political realities awaiting him as president, Lincoln greeted the news of his election with a heavy attitude of deep realization of the responsibilities which had been deposited upon his shoulders. Reportedly, his only comment on receiving the news was, "I feel a great responsibility. God help me, God help me."

Before the Inauguration

Lincoln had to assume a leadership role in his party long before he officially took office. His inauguration would not take place until March of 1861, and the southern states were declaring their intention to secede before this event took place. It was not yet clear to anyone where their secession should be opposed or whether they should be allowed to depart peacefully. After all, the American colonies had chosen to separate from England, and some people, even in the north and the west, felt that it was consistent with the rights of Americans to allow anyone who felt that their government no longer answered their needs to form a government of their own. Some believed that the defection of the southern states was nothing less than the basest treason. Others felt that the southerners were threatening secession merely as a means of attempting to frighten Lincoln into accepting the southern wish to expand the domain of slavery. Everyone wished to avoid a war, if possible, but it would depend entirely on how the new administration chose to view the secession.

Lincoln opposed secession from the beginning, and if war was the inevitable result, then he was willing to go to war. His reasoning was that the slavery question was bound to provoke a violent national conflict eventually, and that "it wouldn't be brave of us to leave this question to be settled by posterity." A strong argument could be made that this was precisely what the Revolutionary generation had done eighty years before; many of the nation's founders had argued strongly that slavery was inconsistent with the democratic principles America was founded on, and that it must be done away with. Only the intransigence of the southern states, who refused to ratify the Constitution until certain anti slavery sections were removed, prevented this from becoming a reality. Lincoln, who was a dilettante student of Revolutionary history, may have been influenced by their example in choosing to settle the slavery issue for his own time.

As Lincoln's long time law partner and intimate friend William Herndon remarked, Lincoln was prepared to "make a grave yard of the South, if rebellion or treason lifts its head: he will execute the laws, as against Treason & Rebellion." At the time, it was widely believed in both the north and the south that war, if it did break out, would be brief, and the casualties minor. The next six years would prove that assumption tragically mistaken.

Chapter Six: President Lincoln: The First Term 1861-1864

Inauguration

Lincoln made the final leg of his journey to the White House with as little pomp and circumstance as he could manage, somewhat to the mortification of his supporters, who wanted to celebrate his coming with great fanfare. It was considered a sign of cowardice by some. But Lincoln was as president as he had been all his life: a deeply modest person, and a man of country manners who did not enjoy or understand the nuances of courtly society behavior.

Lincoln wrote his first Inaugural Address in Springfield, shortly after learning of his election. He showed the speech to members of his cabinet, including his Secretary of State William Seward, formerly his opponent for the Republican nomination. The intention of the speech to reconcile southerners and to attempt to persuade them not to secede. It was not successful, but the speech's closing passage is the most famous of all Lincoln's public remarks, with the exception of the Gettysburg Address:

"My countrymen, one and all, think calmly and *well*, upon this whole subject. Nothing valuable can be lost by taking time. If there be an object to *hurry* any of you, in hot haste, to a step which you would never take *deliberately,* that object will be frustrated by taking time; but no good object can be frustrated by it. Such of you as are now dissatisfied still have the old Constitution unimpaired, and, on the sensitive point, the laws of your own framing under it; while the new administration will have no immediate power, if it would, to change either. If it were admitted that you who are dissatisfied, hold the right side in the dispute, there still is no single good reason for precipitate action. Intelligence, patriotism, Christianity, and a firm reliance on Him, who has never yet forsaken this favored land, are still competent to adjust, in the best way, all our present difficulty.

"In *your* hands, my dissatisfied fellow countrymen, and not in *mine,* is the momentous issue of civil war. The government will not assail *you.* You can have no conflict without being yourselves the aggressors. *You* have no oath registered in Heaven to destroy the government, while *I* shall have the most solemn one to 'preserve, protect, and defend it.'

"I am loath to close. We are not enemies, but friends. We must not be enemies. Though passion may have strained, it must not break our bonds of affection. The mystic chords of memory, stretching from every battle-field, and patriot grave, to every living heart and hearthstone, all over this broad land, will yet swell the chorus of the Union, when again touched, as surely they will be, by the better angels of our nature."

Outbreak of the Civil War

On December 20, 1860, South Carolina announced that it would secede from the Union. The secession of the South came as no surprise to anyone, but complicating the issue was the fact that the south expected to keep the military bases and supplies belonging to the Union that were located in Confederate states. One such base was Fort Sumter, located near Charleston, one of the South's most crucial port cities. When rebel leaders demanded that Union soldiers leave their posts, U.S. Army Major Robert Anderson moved his command from Fort Moultrie to Fort Sumter, which commanded all of Charleston Harbor. All other Union, or Federal, property in South Carolina had already been seized, and Fort Sumter stood alone as the last outpost of the Union government.

The day that Lincoln took office, he learned that Major Anderson had only six weeks' supplies remaining, and was desperately in need of relief from the army. When the new President Lincoln informed the governor of South Carolina that he intended to send a ship to relieve Major Anderson, the governor gave Anderson formal notice to evacuate, which he refused to do. On April 12, 1861, Confederate forces under General Pierre Beauregard ordered his forces to fire on Fort Sumter; there were no casualties, and Anderson was forced to evacuate. This exchange of fire is considered to be the opening event of the Civil War.

South Carolina was the first state to secede from the Union; after the Battle of Fort Sumter six more states quickly followed. Near the end of

Civil War, Lincoln commented on this first outbreak of hostilities: "Both parties deprecated war, but one of them would make war rather than let the nation survive, and the other would accept war rather than let it perish, and the war came."

The Death of Willie Lincoln

On February 20, 1862, the third son of Abraham and Mary Todd Lincoln, William Wallace Lincoln, known as Willie, died at the White House.

The war, which would dominate the entirety of Lincoln's presidency (and thus, the rest of his life), was going badly. The Confederate army was under the command of the former commander of West Point, General Robert E. Lee, a brilliant soldier and tactician who had been offered the command of the Union army. Lee had refused command, because, as a Virginian, he felt that he owed his first loyalty to his home state. It was a blow that the Union would reel from for more than half of the war's duration, as Lee began an aggressive campaign pushing northward into Union territory, where he all but routed the less capable, badly unprepared Union generals.

Lincoln's popularity was on the wane due to the poor performance of the Union army. But early in 1862, his mind was on other matters: the younger two of his three surviving sons, Tad and Willie, had fallen ill. (His oldest son, Robert, was away at college, and his second son, Eddy, had died in Springfield at the age of three.) It is now known that the Lincoln boys probably contracted typhus, which was spread by contaminated water—the water used by the White House came from the Potomac River, and was also used by all the men and horses of the Union army that were camped alongside. Tad's illness was not as severe, but Willie's life was feared for from the beginning.

For Mary Todd Lincoln, Willie's death was a disaster. Her mental health, which had never been robust, was almost unhinged by the loss; reportedly, Lincoln had to threaten her with incarceration in an insane asylum if she could not control her grief. Lincoln's reaction was more restrained, but there was no question that he was profoundly affected. He wept at Willie's bedside, and for a short time, the death seriously impacted the conduct of business at the White House. Lincoln was unable to write any correspondence for several days, and he did not venture from home for more than three weeks.

Lincoln's sole comment in the moments after his son's passing was, "My poor boy, he was too good for this earth. God has called him home. I know that he is much better off in heaven, but then we loved him so. It is hard, hard to have him die!"

Battle of Antietam

The war continued to go badly for the Union, and for the first year and a half of conflict there was scarcely a moment's relief for those who hoped to preserve the Union. As Lincoln put it, the South had been preparing mentally and materially to secede and to defend its secession for the last thirty years, while the Union had a new president and a series of inept generals at its helm. After the Battle of Fort Sumter, Lincoln called for 75,000 volunteers to make up the new Union army. As the first president to oversee a war fought on American soil since James Madison in the War of 1812, Lincoln expanded the president's executive powers to an unprecedented decree, taking full command of the army, blockading every southern port city, and jailing any person suspected of acting as a spy for the south. His first Secretary of War, Simon Cameron, he was obliged to dismiss on charges of corruption and war profiteering. Lincoln replaced him with Edwin Stanton, who was a Democrat, but whom Lincoln trusted more than most Republicans.

The first significant military victory of the Civil War for the Union, and thus for Lincoln, was the Battle of Antietam, also known as the Battle of Sharpsburg, which took place near Sharpsburg, Maryland, on September 17, 1862. Because the south had been victorious for so many months, Confederate General Robert E. Lee had pushed the campaign north into Union territory; there were many Confederate sympathizers in Maryland, and he had hopes of conquering the state. Confederate president Jefferson David was hoping to gain the support of a foreign ally, such as Great Britain, and felt that if the South demonstrated its viability by successfully capturing enemy territory, such an alliance would be more forthcoming. It was, again, a strategy which the American colonies had successfully employed when attempting to gain French support for the Revolution.

Emboldened by their victories at the Battle of Bull Run, Lee's men advanced into Maryland, and Union general George McLellan moved to intercept them. Two of McClellan's officers found a mislaid copy of Lee's battle plans, which enabled McLellan to send troops to head off each of the three southern divisions. The number of Union fatalities was higher than the number of Confederate fatalities, but the strategic victory belonged to the Union. Lincoln had not yet ceased to be disappointed in his generals, however; despite the firm instruction of both Lincoln and Secretary of War Edwin Stanton, General McClellan failed to pursue Lee's forces south after the battle. Lincoln relieved McClellan of his command as a result. The Confederate defeat at Antietam brought an end to the Maryland Campaign, Lee's first systematic attempt to invade northern territory.

The Emancipation Proclamation

The first measure which Lincoln had taken to strike at Southern slave holders as president was the Confiscation Act of 1862, which held that the slaves of any master in rebellion against the Union were free according to the laws of the Union. Around the same time, Lincoln asked Congress to pass an order declaring that it was illegal for any Union officer to return a runaway slave to their Confederate master, thereby contravening the Fugitive Slave Act of 1850. However, Lincoln's position on slavery in the South was the same as what it had always been: as president, he did not have the legal authority to declare slavery to be abolished in the southern states. That power lay in the hands of southern voters.

However, the outbreak of war had placed Lincoln in an interesting legal position. What he could not do as president, he might do as commander-in-chief of the armed forces, provided he could devise a military pretext or justification for the order. Thus, the Emancipation Proclamation came to be written. Because the Proclamation was issued under Lincoln's war powers, it had an expressly military goal: to weaken the Confederacy by depriving them of the slaves that constituted their vast unpaid labor force. Any slave who could get away from their masters and make it to Union lines was automatically free; and because their masters were largely away fighting for the Confederacy, few slave owners had the manpower or weaponry to fight to keep them. The military nature of the order meant, however, that it could not be extended to any slave owner who was not in rebellion against the

Union. This applied to the "border states" of Maryland, Delaware, Kentucky, and Missouri, and also to Tennessee, which had joined the southern states in seceding, but had quickly been occupied by Union forces and was, at the time the Proclamation was issue, ruled by a Union government.

Those who had known Lincoln for a long time and were familiar with his career and his writings knew that his personal wish to put an end to slavery was so strong that he was bound to take advantage of any opportunity to do so that did not jeopardize his equally strong conviction to do only what Constitutionally permissible. But around the time the Emancipation Proclamation was issued, Lincoln began to position himself carefully as being interested solely in preserving the Union, to the point of near indifference on the slavery question:

"If there be those who would not save the Union, unless they could at the same time save slavery, I do not agree with them. If there be those who would not save the Union unless they could at the same time destroy slavery, I do not agree with them. My paramount object in this struggle is to save the Union, and is not either to save or to destroy slavery. If I could save the Union without freeing any slave I would do it, and if I could save it by freeing all the slaves I would do it; and if I could save it by freeing some and leaving others alone I would also do that. What I do about slavery, and the colored race, I do because I believe it helps to save the Union; and what I forbear, I forbear because I do not believe it would help to save the Union.... I have here stated my purpose according to my view of official duty; and I intend no modification of my oft-expressed personal wish that all men everywhere could be free."

While this was not the final end of slavery in the United States, it was a crucial first step, and did much to fix the sympathies of European countries, where slavery had been outlawed for decades, in favor of the Union. Though Lincoln had composed the Proclamation early in 1862, he did not release it until after the Battle of Antietam; he wanted to wait until after a Union victory, so that it wouldn't appear as if he had only freed the slaves out of desperation to strike at the Confederacy any way he could. The final version of the Emancipation Proclamation was therefore issued on January 1, 1863.

The Battle of Gettysburg and the Gettysburg Address

After two more crushing Union defeats at Fredericksburg in December 1862 and at Chancellorsville in May of 1863, the tide of the Civil War changed on a Pennsylvania battlefield near the town of Gettysburg, from July 1-3, 1863. There, a string of Confederate victories gave way to Union dominance. Lee's army was forced to retreat back into Virginia, thus bringing an end to the Gettysburg Campaign, his second attempt to invade the north and force Washington politicians to release the south and bring the war to an end.

Due to the catastrophic casualties suffered on both sides, the Gettysburg battlefield was dedicated as a national cemetery by a group of lawyers and businessmen living in the town of Gettysburg. They invited Lincoln to come and preside over the opening of the cemetery and give a speech. Lincoln had suffered from deep unpopularity as president during the first few years of his presidency owing to the fact that the war was proceeding badly, and taking much longer than anyone had predicted, but the victory at Gettysburg had changed public opinion in his favor just as it had changed the Union's fortunes in the war. Outpourings of love from the public followed him throughout his time in Gettysburg, prompting a French observer to say that "he lived in every heart".

However, Lincoln was not considered the main speaker of the day. He was present merely to lend solemnity to the occasion and give very brief remarks, before a much longer speech was given by a famous public speaker named Edward Everett. Most of those attending the dedication ceremony were the mothers, fathers, wives, and children of the men who had been killed in the battle; some had come to retrieve bodies and take them home to be buried. In total, there were some 15,000 people in attendance at the dedication ceremony.

"Four score and seven years ago our fathers brought forth on this continent a new nation, conceived in liberty, and dedicated to the proposition that all men are created equal.

"Now we are engaged in a great civil war, testing whether that nation, or any nation so conceived and so dedicated, can long endure. We are met on a great battlefield of that war. We have come to dedicate a portion of that field, as a final resting place for those who here gave their lives that that nation might live. It is altogether fitting and proper that we should do this.

"But, in a larger sense, we can not dedicate, we can not consecrate, we can not hallow this ground. The brave men, living and dead, who struggled here, have consecrated it, far above our poor power to add or detract. The world will little note, nor long remember what we say here, but it can never forget what they did here. It is for us the living, rather, to be dedicated here to the unfinished work which they who fought here have thus far so nobly advanced. It is rather for us to be here dedicated to the great task remaining before us—that from these honored dead we take increased devotion to that cause for which they gave the last full measure of devotion—that we here highly resolve that these dead shall not have died in vain—that this nation, under God, shall have a new birth of freedom—and that government of the people, by the people, for the people, shall not perish from the earth."

It only took Lincoln two minutes to deliver this address, following Everett's extremely longwinded and "cold" speech, and it was met by thunderous applause from his audience. In this short speech, Lincoln alludes to reframing the purpose of the Civil War—by mentioning a "new birth of freedom" in the final lines, he explicitly moves the abolition of slavery into the foreground of his priorities. While preserving the Union remained his first task, the Union that would emerge after the end of the war would be one without slavery.

Re-election and Second Inaugural Address

As had happened with General George McClellan, who refused to pursue Lee's retreating army after the Battle of Antietam, Union General George Meade failed to pursue Lee's forces after the Battle of Gettysburg, thereby losing an opportunity to hasten the war's end. By 1864, Lincoln had replaced Meade with General Ulysses S. Grant, future president of the United States, whom Lincoln defended against his detractors by saying that even when he lost battles, still "he fights". Grant was to take command of all Union armies under the rank of Lieutenant General, a rank last held by George Washington when he was head of the American army from the end of his second presidential term until his death. Meanwhile Lincoln also appointed General William Sherman as the commander of Union forces west of the Mississippi.

Grant and Sherman began a coordinated attack intended to rout Confederate forces once and for all, with Grant pitched against Lee's Army of Northern Virginia and Sherman pursuing Johnston's army in Atlanta. Victory for the Union was, from this point, only a matter of time. Sherman captured Atlanta shortly before Lincoln's bid for re-election. His opponent was the Democratic nominee George McLellan, the very general he had dismissed after the Battle of Antietam. For a time, Lincoln's re-election prospects looked grim, as Grant failed to achieve immediate victory. In the interim, Lincoln signed a pledge, which he placed in a sealed envelope and asked his cabinet to sign, stating that if he were not re-elected, he would work with the President-elect to bring the war to an end before his inauguration. However, thanks to the energetic efforts of his party, Lincoln was elected in a landslide. By the time of Lincoln's second inauguration, the Civil War was nearing its end.

The final lines of Lincoln's second inaugural address are famous, particularly the phrase "with malice toward none, with charity toward all", with which Lincoln declared the policy he wished to pursue regarding clemency for the South after the war. But in another part of the address, he speaks explicitly on the subject of slavery, and removes any doubt that the war was fought over that issue.

"Both read the same Bible and pray to the same God, and each invokes His aid against the other. It may seem strange that any men should dare to ask a just God's assistance in wringing their bread from the sweat of other men's faces, but let us judge not, that we be not judged. The prayers of both could not be answered. That of neither has been answered fully. The Almighty has His own purposes. "Woe unto the world because of offenses; for it must needs be that offenses come, but woe to that man by whom the offense cometh." If we shall suppose that American slavery is one of those offenses which, in the providence of God, must needs come, but which, having continued through His appointed time, He now wills to remove, and that He gives to both North and South this terrible war as the woe due to those by whom the offense came, shall we discern therein any departure from those divine attributes which the believers in a living God always ascribe to Him? Fondly do we hope, fervently do we pray, that this mighty scourge of war may speedily pass away. Yet, if God wills that it continue until all the wealth piled by the bondsman's two hundred and fifty years of unrequited toil shall be sunk, and until every drop of blood drawn with the lash shall be paid by another drawn with the sword, as was said three thousand years ago, so still it must be said "the judgements of the Lord are true and righteous altogether."

In this passage, Lincoln avoids laying the blame for the war directly on the shoulders of the Confederacy, but holds the war as a judgment visited by God on both the north and the south. This was the attitude with which Lincoln was to approach Reconstruction.

The Passing of the Thirteenth Amendment

The Emancipation Proclamation had not abolished slavery everywhere, nor had it made slavery itself illegal; it had merely freed the slaves of Confederate masters as a war measure to weaken the south's economy. The Thirteenth Amendment, however, which was passed by both houses of Congress on January 31, 1865, abolished slavery, defined as involuntary servitude, in the United States.

This is the full text of the amendment:

"**Section 1.** Neither slavery nor involuntary servitude, except as a punishment for crime whereof the party shall have been duly convicted, shall exist within the United States, or any place subject to their jurisdiction.

Section 2. Congress shall have power to enforce this article by appropriate legislation."

The amendment was hotly contested in the House of Representatives. Radical Republican and famed abolitionist James Mitchell Ashley originally proposed the amendment in 1863. Those who opposed the amendment did so on the grounds that it would eventually lead to full citizenship and voting rights for blacks. Lincoln was not necessarily in favor of either of those eventualities, but he was concerned that because the Emancipation Proclamation had been issued under his expanded war time powers that it would be reversed once the war was over. Regarding this concern, he stated that, "If the people should, by whatever mode or means, make it an Executive duty to re-enslave such persons, another, and not I, must be their instrument to perform it."

Getting the Thirteenth Amendment passed was Lincoln's first priority after he was re-elected in 1864. He considered the fact of his re-election to be a sign that the majority of American voters supported the measure. Lincoln engaged in some of the most devious political maneuvers of his career to gain the necessary number of votes for the amendment to pass in the House, going so far as to authorize William Seward, his Secretary of State, to resort to bribery and patronage rewards in exchange for the promise of votes. Lincoln believed, or at least argued, that the war, which was nearing its close but not yet with a specific end date in sight, would be shortened by the passage of the Thirteenth Amendment, namely because it would remove, once and for all, any hope that the Confederacy might by clinging to that by continuing to fight, it could preserve the right to keep slavery legal. This was not an idle fear on Lincoln's part; the four border states, where slavery remained legal even after the Emancipation Proclamation, fought vehemently for slavery, and were considered allies to the South on that specific issue.

As the hour of the vote drew near on January 31, members of the House began debating a rumor that had reached the that emissaries from the Confederacy had come to Washington to initiate peace talks, which raised hopes that perhaps the war could be ended without slavery having to be abolished. Confederate emissaries were, in fact, on their way to Washington for this exact purpose, but Lincoln sent a message to Congress stating that, "So far as I know, there are no peace commissioners in the city, or likely to be in it." This was, if not an outright lie, certainly an evasion of the truth; the phrase "as far as I know" was nothing less than an evasion such as a prevaricating witness might use when giving testimony, as Lincoln the lawyer knew full well. But Lincoln was determined that the amendment should pass, and did not hesitate to use a certain measure of deceit to make it happen.

The Thirteenth Amendment passed the House by a very narrow margin. When the final vote was tallied, loud cheers were heard in the House chamber, including the voices of free blacks who had come to witness the amendment's passing. Lincoln added his signature to the Thirteenth Amendment on February 1, 1865, making it the only amendment ever to be signed by a president after it had already secured the necessary number of votes in Congress.

According to one of Lincoln's associates, news of the amendment's passing "filled [Lincoln's] heart with joy, for he saw in it the complete consummation of his own work."

Assassination and Death of Abraham Lincoln

On April 9, 1865, General Robert E. Lee surrendered to General Ulysses S. Grant at Appomattox, Virginia, thus bringing an end to the Civil War. To Harriet Beecher Stowe, author of *Uncle Tom's Cabin,* one of the seminal abolitionist texts which stirred up pro-Union feeling for the war, Lincoln observed, "Whichever way it [the war] ends, I have the impression that I sha'n't last long after it's over."

Lincoln's chief concern after the war was Reconstruction: rebuilding the south so that it could recover from the ravages of the war fought on its own soil, and integrating the newly free black population so that they had a place in the new society and the means to make a living. Lincoln had debated, and rejected, the prospect of subjecting the south to any punitive measures as punishment for rebellion. This was in direct opposition to many Radical Republicans, who felt that by seceding from the Union, the Confederate South had rejected its own status as a state, and reverted to the status of a territory, meaning that it had no right of self governance or representation in Congress. Lincoln felt that this would only exacerbate the damage; he wanted things in the south to go back to normal as quickly as possible. Lincoln's vice president, "War Democrat" Andrew Johnson, believed that "treason must be made odious"—that is, that some measure of punishment was in order for the southern states. After Lincoln's death, the bulk of the work of reconstruction would, of course, be left to Johnson to do, as his successor.

The last project that Lincoln seems to have been turning his attention to before his death, as part of Reconstruction, was enfranchisement—voting rights—for blacks. On his way back to Washington from meeting Grant at Richmond, Lincoln gave a speech which hinted at this intention. Such noted abolitionists as Frederick Douglass, a free black man and one of the most brilliant writers of his generation, believed that

Lincoln was sincere and committed to enfranchisement for blacks. So, apparently, did his future assassin: John Wilkes Booth was in the audience for this speech. Reportedly, Wilkes remarked to a companion, "That means nigger citizenship [...] That is the last speech he will ever make."

During Lincoln's last cabinet meeting, his cabinet officers remarked that an enormous weight seemed to have been lifted from him; the Treasury Secretary said that he "never saw Mr. Lincoln so cheerful and happy." His wife made a similar comment, noting that Lincoln was more cheerful than she was used to seeing him, and he replied, "And well I may feel so, Mary; for I consider this day the war has come to a close. We must both be more cheerful in the future. Between the war and the loss of our darling Willie we have been very miserable."

On April 14, 1865, Abraham Lincoln escorted his wife to Ford's Theater to attend a performance of a play called "Our American Cousin." General Ulysses S. Grant and his wife had been invited to accompany them, but had declined the invitation because Julia Grant did not care for the company of Mary Todd Lincoln. Secretary of War Edwin Stanton advised Lincoln not to go to the theater, or anywhere else public and exposed, because he was afraid of assassination attempts. Lincoln did have bodyguards, but they did not accompany him everywhere, and he particularly requested that they not go to the theater with him. Lincoln had received regular threats against his life since he was first elected, and in fact had a special file set aside just for "assassination letters". The fact of the matter was, no American president, or even high official, had ever been assassinated before; it was considered a European custom, not consistent with the character of a democracy. This was in spite of the fact that Lincoln had been the target of an assassination attempt at least once before, in 1864—though the gunman had only succeeded in shooting his hat.

John Wilkes Booth was an out of work actor who had been fixated on Lincoln for some time. He had devised a plan to kidnap the president the previous year, but his co-conspirators had failed to play their part. On the night of April 14, 1865, he intended to assassinated not only Lincoln, but Vice President Andrew Johnson and Secretary of State William Seward. Supposedly, Booth felt guilty because he had promised his mother not to join the Confederate army, and after Lee surrendered, he felt that he had not done his part. Booth was professionally associated with Ford's Theater, and it was largely a coincidence that he happened to hear of Lincoln's plan to attend the performance that evening. His decision to commit the murder was a crime of opportunity. Booth's principle motivation was undoubtedly his avowed hatred of freedom and equality for blacks, and his life-long desire to be famous. He was, reportedly, confused by the fact that the newspapers excoriated rather than praised him after the assassination.

At about 10:30 p.m., Booth slipped into the president's theater box, jammed the door shut behind him, and shot him in the back of the head. Major Rathbone, who had accompanied the Lincolns to the theater along with his fiancée, attempted to restrain him, but Booth slashed at his arm with a knife and jumped from the box to the stage, where he was helped to escape by his co-conspirators from the earlier kidnapping plot.

Lincoln lived another nine hours, though he never regained consciousness. Once it was understood that the President had been shot, three doctors in the audience rushed toward his box to try and help him. These doctors made the decision to take him to a boardinghouse across the street from the theater, for fear that he would not survive being transported back to the White house. His wife, sons, and various officials joined the deathbed scene throughout the night. Mary Todd Lincoln was inconsolable; she frequently expressed the wish that Booth had shot her as well.

Abraham Lincoln died at 7:22 a.m. on April 15, 1865. Secretary of War Edwin Stanton, who had stood by his bed throughout the night, was heard to say, "Now he belongs to the ages."

Historian Michael Burlingame offers a final anecdote of Lincoln family life. The day after Lincoln's death, Tad Lincoln asked a family visitor whether they believed that his father had gone to heaven. The visitor replied that they were sure that he had, to which Tad replied, "Then I am glad he has gone there, for he never was happy after he came here. This was not a good place for him."

On April 18, Lincoln's body was arranged to lie in state in the East Room of the White House; some 20,000 members of the public came to see him and pay their last respects. His funeral took place on the next day, April 19, 1865—the anniversary of the beginning of both the Revolutionary War and the Civil War. Afterwards, the coffin of Lincoln's son Willie was exhumed from its grave, and it joined Lincoln's coffin on a procession by train across the country to Springfield, Illinois, where it was finally buried.

Legendary American poet Walt Whitman wrote the poem "When Lilacs Last In the Dooryard Bloom'd" about his experience viewing Lincoln's funeral procession.

Coffin that passes through lanes and streets,

Through day and night with the great cloud darkening the land,

With the pomp of the inloop'd flags with the cities draped in black,

With the show of the States themselves as of crape-veil'd women standing,

With processions long and winding and the flambeaus of the night,

With the countless torches lit, with the silent sea of faces and the unbared heads,

With the waiting depot, the arriving coffin, and the sombre faces,

With dirges through the night, with the thousand voices rising strong and solemn,

With all the mournful voices of the dirges pour'd around the coffin,

The dim-lit churches and the shuddering organs—where amid these you journey,

With the tolling tolling bells' perpetual clang,

Here, coffin that slowly passes,

I give you my sprig of lilac.

Conclusion

Just as Abraham Lincoln would be the last person to suggest that his life story was proper material for myth making, he would be—he *was*—the last person who would call himself an abolitionist. This is, perhaps, the single aspect of his legacy that is remembered most vividly, and understood most poorly. That Lincoln is the president who freed the slaves is beyond cavil; what his feelings about slavery were is often guessed at; but his actual politics regarding slavery would come as a surprise to most people, if they were widely understood.

Lincoln's first exposure to slavery was probably during the river boat trip he made to New Orleans in 1829, while he was still effectively his father's indentured servant. He wrote many years afterwards of seeing slaves at auction for the first time; the naïve young man witnessed naked black women, some of them very young girls, being probed and prodded by prospective male buyers. Lincoln found the sight sickening, and from this encounter he took home the conviction that slavery was a hideous, evil business. But it was one thing to consider a slave auction disgusting and quite another to pronounce oneself an abolitionist and take up the banner of emancipation. Very few white people were abolitionists in the 1830's. Slavery was not universally popular; it was illegal in half of the country. But abolitionists—that is, reformers who considered slavery not just evil, but a sin, and believed that slavery should be abolished instantly and without condition—were radicals. Even when their methods of protest were peaceful, they were hated and feared by the vast majority of people. The popular belief in the early nineteenth century was that abolitionist rhetoric did nothing but encourage slaves in the south to rise up against their white owners and massacre them. It is difficult to exaggerate how frightened white slave owners were of such uprisings, and how paranoid they were of their becoming a reality. Abolitionists, accordingly, were considered enemies of law and order, sowers of discord—anarchists, in a word. Lincoln himself believed that abolitionists were troublemakers, and that they actually increased the sufferings of slaves, because the more the white slave owners grew to fear a slave revolt, the more harshly they treated them. It is possible that he had a point.

How then does a talented politician with a morally rooted and viscerally emotional dislike of slavery contend with the slavery issue over the course of his political career—particularly in a state such as Illinois, where slavery was illegal, but where the large population of transplanted southerners insured that, on any voting issue, there would be considerable solidarity with and support for the interests of the slave states? In Lincoln's case, he approached the question like a lawyer. The laws of the land must reign supreme, and the rights of property owners must be upheld, even when their property was human beings. The abolitionists could not be given what they wanted—an immediate end to slavery, imposed by the authority of the federal government, whether the voters of the slave states liked it or not—without violating the most fundamental precept of the Constitution, the very issue over which the American colonies had revolted against British rule less than eighty years before: that no laws would be made without the consent of the people whom the laws affected.

In other words, Lincoln felt that so long as slavery was legally permitted by the Constitution, the rights of slave owners must be upheld. To abolish slavery by fiat would result in war and bloodshed, as slave owners desperately tried to control the people they had enslaved, and the south as a political body finally did what it had long been threatening to do, and seceded from the union. Abolishing slavery in a way that did not lead to the immediate upending of law and order would require the consent of the slave owners—a prospect that sounds so impossible to modern ears that it could be mistaken for the lead in to a joke. But a number of politicians, including Lincoln, attempted this at the state level in the decade prior to the Civil War. During Lincoln's sole term in the House of Representatives, he authored a resolution that would bring a gradual end to slavery in the District of Columbia, by declaring that the children of slave mothers born after a certain date were born free, and offering market value compensation to the owner of any slaves willing to free them immediately. This resolution was defeated, as was every reform of its kind attempted throughout the country. But it demonstrates that Lincoln believed that a peaceful, political end to slavery was possible.

How deeply did Lincoln's antipathy to slavery run? He felt strongly enough about it that as a member of the Illinois General Assembly he authored an anti slavery resolution—nothing earth shattering, just a protest to another resolution the assembly had already passed, which was in itself only a statement of solidarity with the southern slave states. But it stands out as the only anti slavery legislation of any kind seen by the Illinois assembly that year, or for many years after. It stands out even more for the fact that Lincoln could only persuade one other delegate to the assembly to sign the resolution with him.

Lincoln was a brilliant politician, but after the first shots were fired at Ft. Sumter in South Carolina, signaling the beginning of the Civil War, he had a very different situation on his hands where the slavery issue was concerned. Always, he had attempted to pursue legal (that is, Constitutional) means to bring an end to slavery; but the very people whose right to a vote on the subject he had been trying to preserve had seceded from the Union. This put Lincoln, as president, in a rare position. In the Emancipation Proclamation of 1863, Lincoln declared all slaves living in the Confederate states to be free, meaning that if they managed to escape their owners and find their way to Union lines, no one could return them to their masters, despite the provisions of the Fugitive Slave Act. The Emancipation Proclamation was an executive order—that is, a command given by the president which has the full force of law, and does not have to take the form of a bill to be passed through Congress.

Executive orders are a somewhat mysterious aspect of American government. They are not explicitly provided for in the Constitution, and they are limited more by tradition than by law. American presidents are generally supposed to work with and through Congress, so as to insure that the American people are being governed by their consent—or at least, the consent of their elected representatives. Lincoln, therefore, was taking a certain degree of risk onto himself by essentially freeing slave in the south on his own responsibility.

But the Emancipation Proclamation did not put an end to slavery for once and all. Obviously, part of the reason why Lincoln was able to risk such a sweeping use of his presidential powers was because of the Civil War. Freeing the slaves in the south could be justified as a military action that was calculated to weaken the Confederate states by encouraging their slaves to turn against them, now that they could be sure that permanent freedom awaited them in the north. But if the war had come to an end prior to 1865, it is possible that slavery would have continued to exist. Not all of the slave states were affected by the Emancipation Proclamation. There were still some five hundred thousand slave in Missouri, Kentucky, Delaware, and Maryland, none of which had joined the south in seceding from the Union. Likewise, Tennessee, which had seceded but had been taken back into Union control by 1863, did not fall under the provisions of the Proclamation.

In a strange way, despite the fact that the Civil War was explicitly a war over slavery, it might not necessarily have spelled an end to all slavery in the United States. The fact that it did so can be attributed largely to the fact that Abraham Lincoln was determined to end it. That was why, between 1864 and 1865, Lincoln supported the Thirteenth Amendment, authored by representative James Mitchell Ashley. The Thirteenth Amendment abolished slavery in the United States for good; it settled the freedom of enslaved black people residing in the border states, the frontier territories, and any future state to join the Union. The children of black men and women freed by the Emancipation Proclamation could not be sold back into slavery, as many abolitionists feared would happen after the war. Many dire issues regarding the fate of free black people in the United States remained unsettled, but freedom, Lincoln knew, must come first.

So was Abraham Lincoln, then, everything that following generations have made him out to be— a reforming pioneer, an American hero, the best president the country has ever had, a patron saint of liberty? Possibly; it might almost depend on who you asked. As with George Washington, and every distant historical figure that Americans have seized upon as a national hero, the legacy that has been imposed on Lincoln reflects what Americans have wished to believe to be true about their own past. Any inconvenient fact that does not fit the image tends to fade out of popular memory, becoming a relic that lives only for academics and committed students of history.

One example of an uncomfortable fact which has all but disappeared from the popular narrative of Lincoln as champion of liberty is Lincoln's ideas regarding what should become of "free negroes" after they were no longer slaves. The question of where former slaves would live, what rights they would be given, and how to control them was deeply intertwined with the larger conversation about the slavery issue. Whites, even those who regarded slavery as an evil, were deeply anxious about the prospect of free black people moving to their cities in large numbers. The presence of a free black population, especially a visible one, was considered a disgrace, a sign that a city had gone to the dogs—like litter on the streets.

The fact that Lincoln freed the slaves has inclined us to think of him as possessing very nearly modern attitudes about racial equality. In reality, the only thing considered more extreme than abolitionism in mid nineteenth century America was a belief in racial equality—and at no point in Lincoln's life or career could he have been called an extremist. Lincoln believed that black Americans were entitled to full legal equality—that is, that the same legal protections that applied to white should apply to blacks. He did not believe in racial equality

Only a vanishingly small number of the white politicians and activists who opposed slavery took the extra step of espousing a belief in racial equality. It was taken for granted even by the vast majority of abolitionists that black people were intellectually inferior to whites, that their morals were suspect, that they lacked ambition, and that they would rather be poor and lazy than work hard and be prosperous. Lincoln had serious doubts about the ability of free blacks to integrate peacefully into white society (or at least, white society's ability to permit free blacks to integrate without violent retaliation). The resolution which Lincoln authored while serving in the House of Representatives, proposing an end to slavery in the District of Columbia, contained the first iteration of a plan for "dealing" with a free black population that Lincoln would return to from time to time until his death: colonization. The plan Lincoln presented to Congress suggested that wealthy donors would make funds available to any free black person who was interested in leaving the

United States to settle overseas. He returned to this plan once he was president, going so far as to meet with a black delegation and attempt to convince them that emigration, whether to Liberia, in Africa, or to the Dutch colony of Surinam, or the British colony now known as Belize, constituted their best chance of peace and happiness after the war.

It is perhaps worth noting that Lincoln's plans supporting colonization were largely abandoned once he had issued the Emancipation Proclamation, which allowed blacks to enlist in the military. As one historian has noted, once a president had asked black men to fight for their country, he could no longer claim that it was not theirs.

During any discussion like this one, in which the reality of Lincoln's views and policies are held up for comparison against the legend that has grown in his wake, many people stand ready to proclaim that is not fair to hold any person of

Lincoln's era accountable for racist views. There seems to be a feeling that a person living in the nineteenth century scarcely had any choice as to whether or not their views would seem backwards or offensive to persons living in the twenty first century. But this feeling fails to take into account the fact that there were persons of Lincoln's era—men who served as his colleagues and subordinates, and to whose views and opinions Lincoln was continually exposed—who did believe in racial equality. In other words, non racist perspectives were not, as some people would have use believe, completely inaccessible one hundred and fifty years ago. It simply took greater courage, and greater willingness to stand out from the crowd back then than it does now.

So our consensus, perhaps, is that Abraham Lincoln was not a saint (although after his assassination his reputation as a martyr was inevitable). Nor was he prophetically far sighted, or gifted with a superhuman ability to transcend the limitations of his era. But do we really need him to be? Lincoln avoided being associated with abolitionism, not from any desire to support slavery, but because he believed that abolitionism could never succeed in bringing slavery to an end. The abolitionist would say, perhaps, that the slave who was living in bondage could not bear to wait for the machinery of politics to deliver her, and open war could scarcely make her lot in life worse than it already was—and no doubt the abolitionist was right. But Lincoln, the plain spoken, tough minded, canny politician succeeded in freeing the slaves where the abolitionists had failed. His attitude towards race was not as enlightened as some others. But his politics were guided by sound principles, namely the belief that everyone deserved a fair shot at the rights guaranteed by the Constitution—life, liberty, and the pursuit of happiness. Abraham Lincoln was not a saint, but could a saint, one wonders, have become president?

There is no getting past one fact of Abraham Lincoln's life and legacy: in the end, he freed the slaves because he believed that it was right to do so. Lincoln was well aware that many people, even in the north, even among those loyal to the union, did not relish the idea of freeing the slaves and having to deal with free blacks competing with whites for jobs, or any of the other benefits of society. He too regarded that prospect with distaste, but ultimately he felt that bringing a final end to slavery in his lifetime was more important than any inconvenience that would arise from it. How much Lincoln wanted to end slavery is evident from the lengths he went to in order to get the Thirteenth Amendment passed. It required all of his considerable talents as a political deal maker, and all of powers of deception. Where did deception come into it? Lincoln was able to garner popular support for the Thirteenth Amendment because it was believed that passing the amendment would deal a mortal blow to the south, and thus hasten the end of the war. But in fact, Lincoln was already in peace talks with Jefferson Davis's Confederate government before the Thirteenth Amendment came to be debated in Congress. He concealed this fact from everyone but a few trusted associates, knowing that if Congress believed there was a chance of ending the war with some form of slavery still intact, that was the option they would prefer. Even many of those who opposed slavery felt that the Emancipation Proclamation had gone far enough in that direction.

Lincoln, however, wished it to go further. All throughout his political career, Lincoln gave a certain impression of holding himself back. As a delegate to the Illinois General Assembly, he spent most of his first year sitting back, observing, and studying learning his trade; his time in the House of Representatives gives a similar impression. Before becoming president, Lincoln's politics regarding slavery were founded on the principle that "honey catches more flies than gall". One had to tread carefully, he seems to have felt, in order to strike the most calculated blows at slavery. But this changed to some degree once Lincoln was finally president. For decades, he had been holding himself back and saving himself up. During the run up to the vote on the Thirteenth Amendment, however, when Lincoln's cabinet was scrambling to gather enough support to ensure that the Amendment passed, Lincoln made a statement which reveals that he was keenly aware that his audience was not just the men in the room with him: rather, history itself had its eyes on him.

"I am President of the United States, clothed with great power. The abolition of slavery by Constitutional provisions settles the fate, for all ... time, not only of the millions now in bondage, but of unborn millions to come – a measure of such importance that those two votes must be procured. I leave it to you to determine how it shall be done, but remember that I am President of the United States, clothed with immense power, and I expect you to procure those two votes ..."

Other books available by author on Kindle, paperback and audio

George Washington: First Guardian of American Liberty

Sources Consulted

Burlingame, Michael. *Abraham Lincoln: A Life.* John Hopkins University Press, 2008.

> Retrieved February 12, 2016 at http://www.knox.edu/about-knox/lincoln-studies-center/burlingame-abraham-lincoln-a-life

Goodwin, Doris Kearns. *Team of Rivals: The Political Genius of Abraham Lincoln.* Simon & Schuster, 2006.

Essay announcing Lincoln's candidacy for Illinois Legislature, 1832

http://www.abrahamlincolnonline.org/lincoln/speeches/1832.htm

Lyceum Address

> http://www.abrahamlincolnonline.org/lincoln/speeches/lyceum.htm

Peoria Address

http://quod.lib.umich.edu/cgi/t/text/text-idx?c=lincoln;cc=lincoln;rgn=div2;view=text;idno=lincoln2;node=lincoln2:282.1

Notes for a Law Lecture
http://www.abrahamlincolnonline.org/lincoln/speeches/lawlect.htm

Transcripts of the Lincoln-Douglas debates
http://www.bartleby.com/251/

Lincoln's First Inaugural Address
http://www.abrahamlincolnonline.org/lincoln/speeches/1inaug.htm

Willie Lincoln's Death: A Private Agony for a President Facing a Nation of Pain
https://www.washingtonpost.com/lifestyle/style/willie-lincolns-death-a-private-agony-for-a-president-facing-a-nation-of-pain/2011/09/29/gIQAv7Z7SL_story.html

Made in United States
Orlando, FL
18 January 2023

28812591R00139